# SPA
## FOOD

RECIPES WITH JUDY KNIPE

TEXT WITH LYNNE ROBERTS

PHOTOGRAPHS BY LILO RAYMOND

FOOD STYLING BY ANDREA DEANE

TABLEWARE STYLING BY SAM CROCKER

# SPA FOOD

EDWARD J. SAFDIE

MENUS & RECIPES FROM THE
SONOMA MISSION INN

CLARKSON N. POTTER, INC./PUBLISHERS

DISTRIBUTED BY CROWN PUBLISHERS, INC./NEW YORK

FOR MY WIFE, CARLENE

CLARKSON N. POTTER, INC. AND EDWARD J. SAFDIE
WISH TO THANK AMERICAN AIRLINES
FOR THEIR GENEROUS ASSISTANCE.

**PUBLISHER'S NOTE:** THIS BOOK CONTAINS A DIET PROGRAM
TO BE FOLLOWED BY THE READER IN CONJUNCTION WITH A PROGRAM
OF EXERCISE. HOWEVER, NOT ALL DIETS ARE DESIGNED FOR ALL
INDIVIDUALS. BEFORE STARTING THIS OR ANY OTHER DIET
PROGRAM, YOU SHOULD CONSULT YOUR PHYSICIAN.

Published by Clarkson N. Potter, Inc., 225 Park Avenue South, New York, New York
10003 and simultaneously in Canada by General Publishing Company Limited
**CLARKSON N. POTTER, POTTER,** and colophon are trademarks of Clarkson N. Potter, Inc.

Manufactured in Japan

DESIGN BY GAEL TOWEY DILLON

LIBRARY OF CONGRESS CATALOGING IN PUBLICATION DATA

Safdie, Edward J.
Spa Food.
Includes index.
1. Low-calorie diet—Recipes.
II. Title.
RM222.2.S22   1985      641.5′635      84-28313
ISBN 0-517-55654-5

# CONTENTS

INTRODUCTION
1

THE SPA PROGRAM
8

CLEANSING DAYS/12

850-CALORIE MENUS/20

THE SPA AT HOME
60

1,200-CALORIE MENUS/62

MORE MAIN COURSES/104

MORE DESSERTS/108

BRIEFCASE LUNCHES/112

SPA MENUS FOR
SPECIAL OCCASIONS
116

BRUNCH/120

BARBECUE/124

PICNIC/128

VINEYARD LUNCH/132

BUFFET DINNER/136

COCKTAIL PARTY/140

FALL HOLIDAY DINNER/144

SPA BASICS
152

MAKING IT WORK/154

EXERCISE: A WAY OF LIFE/157

SPA STOCKS AND SAUCES/160

THE SPA KITCHEN/164

INDEX/166

ACKNOWLEDGMENTS/170

Sonoma is a very special part of the world to me. When I drive across San Francisco's Golden Gate Bridge at sunset, the tensions of city life dissolve with the first view of the blue bay below and the rolling hills ahead. I never tire of making this trip to the Inn through the calm countryside, dotted with farmhouses and grazing cows, past the luxuriant California vineyards, along winding roads lined with cypress trees.

In the heart of the wine country, hidden in the valley of Sonoma, is the town of Boyes Hot Springs. There, the Inn is approached through an entranceway of Spanish arches leading to a circular driveway shaded by sycamores and evergreens. The sound of a spring-fed stream creates a relaxed mood. It is a fantasy world, apart from the frenetic pace and pressures of city life—a tranquil hideaway in Spanish-revival style.

Historically, Sonoma was the site of the northernmost mission in California, and the Sonoma Mission Inn draws its name from this heritage. The area of Boyes Hot Springs attracted health seekers from the time the Indians first used the natural sulfur springs as a healing place to the turn of the century when the Boyes Hot Springs Hotel lured voyagers to take the waters in a European-style cure. The hotel burned down in 1923, and the Sonoma Mission Inn was built in 1926.

My first view of the Sonoma Mission Inn was as a child when I was taken there by my parents on a Sunday outing. We returned many times for a day or a longer stay, and I can picture vividly those summer visits. Later, when I began looking for a site for a spa in 1979, I remembered the beauty of the countryside and the comfortable feeling of the old inn. There was a hint of sentimentality in my return. Although the place was in disrepair, I was fortunate to find the owner was ready to sell. It was clear that there was an opportunity to create the luxurious resort and spa I had in mind.

Another appealing aspect in developing the Inn was the opportunity for architectural

restoration, long a subject of interest for me. At the Sonoma Mission Inn, as in all of our spas and inns—the Greenhouse in Texas, the Norwich Inn in Connecticut, and the California Terrace in the Hôtel de Paris in Monaco as well as in our New York City restaurant, Jack's—we work closely with architects and interior designers to restore and conserve the architectural elements from the past. At the Spa, interior designer Charles Swerz helped us renovate its original arched structure.

The Inn's decor, by the late San Francisco designer and close friend John Dickinson, is a blend of European Grand Hotel style and country comfort. By contrast, the Spa, housed in an adjacent building, is almost futuristic, like stepping into the twenty-first century. Following complete renovation, the Inn reopened on a lucky Friday the thirteenth, June 1980. Since then people have come to Sonoma from all parts of the country and abroad, some simply to sample the pleasures of our idyllic setting, others to take part in our renowned Spa program.

Unlike many diet spas, where guests are rigorously segregated, our Spa participants stay at the Inn and mingle with regular visitors. Ours is not an extremist approach. Guests can walk the grounds, meet other guests, relax in the grand lobby, wander into town, play tennis, go horseback riding, visit a local vineyard. The lush setting helps, of course: it's luxurious, tranquil, and designed to be inspirational. The soothing Spa colors were chosen to create an optimistic mood.

Of course, nutritious, beautifully presented food is the bedrock of any spa program, and we are particularly proud of the meals we serve. In developing our menus and recipes with our chef and nutritionist, I found that my own background had provided me with principles of good food and healthful eating that dovetailed neatly with their more technical expertise. Because my father is of European Mediterranean background, the primary diet of our household consisted of whole grains, homemade yogurt, lean poultry and fish, very little meat, and lots of fresh fruits, vegetables, and salads. And in many ways the dishes I grew up on became the precursors to the meals we developed here at the Spa.

In one sense it's not surprising. My father's Old World philosophy was founded on a strong belief in the role of diet and exercise in maintaining good health, and this philosophy was the cornerstone of our meals at home. In the Old World there were no convenience foods; everything was bought fresh and whole. My father loved shopping for food in the open-air markets, where he bought wheat and barley out of big sacks, picked bunches of fresh herbs and strings of garlic hanging from the stalls, and chose ripe fruits from the displays.

We were a family of enthusiastic eaters but not restaurant-goers. Everything was prepared at home. My father acted as executive chef, my American-born mother as sous chef, and all the children participated. In winter, we helped beat the batter for breakfast muffins. In spring, we hulled bushels of fresh strawberries to put up for preserves. For our favorite summer soup, gazpacho, we chopped tomatoes, green peppers, onions, and cucumbers. So I learned the many pleasures of cooking—and eating—at a very young age.

Both my father and my mother had certain firm rules, which have become common-place health practices today. We had only homemade yogurt (often with sliced cucumber and mint leaves), and freshly baked bread from 100 percent stone-ground whole wheat. My father prepared lots of fish, "for the brain," and believed red meat was not good for you. We consumed a large salad at every meal, my father invoking the French idiom "Salad is the broom of the stomach." He loved garlic, a preference to which he attributes the fact that he was rarely sick. He drank two glasses of wine a day "for the circulation." And he always insisted that the family take a stroll after dinner, "to help digestion." Some of his Old World _Excellent_ tricks, such as making a three-egg omelet using only one yolk, are remarkably akin to those employed in nouvelle cuisine. It was, in fact, a simple, healthy, commonsense diet based on much the same principles as those we embrace at the Spa.

When I was grown and on my own, I cooked constantly, as a form of relaxation. I enjoyed the instant gratification and the appreciation of guests. Perhaps I like hosting our hotel guests for some of the same reasons. Today I still prepare for my wife and daughter many of the same dishes my parents served me. And because moderation—not depriva-tion—is the foundation of my cooking beliefs, they have come to appreciate my cooking just as I savored that of my parents.

This same philosophy—you can eat anything in moderation—may explain why our Spa regimen succeeds where others fail. Guests seldom experience a sense of deprivation and austerity. You *can* eat low-calorie, high-nutrition meals and still enjoy yourself. You don't have to go hungry, and you don't have to give up all the foods, wine, or desserts you love. A four-ounce glass of wine with dinner on occasion is not harmful. (My father's belief that it aids digestion, improves circulation, and lowers cholesterol is shared by some doctors.)

Here at the Spa, our fare is an eclectic cuisine of international inspiration that makes for a unique menu. It includes, for instance, an Italian pasta primavera, a French bouillabaisse, eggs spiced with Mexican salsa and chili peppers, a Middle Eastern shish kebab, a simple New England lobster, and Japanese sashimi, as well as classic French soups, soufflés, and sorbets.

Guests are always astonished that our Spa dishes are so flavorful. We do season lav-ishly, but instead of salt we use fresh herbs and spices, peppers and garlic, reductions of lemon and lime juice, and double-rich stocks, reduced twice to intensify their flavors. We thicken our sauces with arrowroot or vegetable purées rather than flour, cream, or butter,

and design our preparations to make the most of each individual ingredient's color, texture, flavor, and aroma.

Our menus emphasize grilling, broiling, roasting, steaming, and poaching. We steam or boil vegetables only until crisp-tender, or serve them raw as hors d'oeuvres or salads. Shorter cooking time preserves more vitamins and minerals.

Each dish is arranged with great attention to presentation—one of the reasons we have included a photograph for each recipe in this book. But cooking and dining should be a complete aesthetic experience, encompassing more than just what is on the plate. It can be a pleasure to go to the market and see the fresh fruits and vegetables. There is a creative satisfaction in handling the ingredients and ordering them on the plate. There is visual enjoyment in the food and the table setting and surroundings.

Nowhere are we more demanding of quality than when it comes to selecting the ingredients for our menus. A supermarket oil bears little resemblance to a high-quality cold-pressed oil; organically raised chicken has a taste and texture that puts the usual bird to shame; fresh crisp spinach will please the palate and the eye more than spinach that has sat for days jammed in its cellophane bag. Coffee (decaf, of course) made from freshly ground beans that have been stored in the freezer is far more aromatic and flavorful than coffee made from canned grounds that have languished for months on a supermarket shelf.

Our chefs are ever on the lookout for quality produce and ingredients and also ever mindful of their freshness. You should be too. You may find the health-food store a good source for unadulterated and thus more flavorful produce, oils, and packaged items. Experiment. Taste. Search out the very best stores, whether they be your local supermarket, gourmet specialty store, ethnic shops, or mail-order catalogs. To help you organize your kitchen to prepare Spa dishes, we've listed what we recommend you keep on hand and also give you our shopping tips for the things you'll need to buy fresh in The Spa Kitchen (page 164).

The menus and recipes in this collection were developed over a three-year period by Escoffier-trained chef Lawrence Elbert, formerly at the Connaught Grill and Savoy Hotel in London, who helped to create the menu at our restaurant in New York City, Jack's, and certified nutritionist Toni Christiansen. These meals demonstrate that low-calorie food can be not only flavorful and filling but also dazzling to look at. While in London, Chef Elbert was inspired by the move toward *cuisine minceur*, a precursor of low-calorie *haute cuisine*, and some of our dishes reflect this influence. But our nutritionist has taken his innovations one step further, devising menus that combine the dishes to provide maximum nutrition and a high and constant release of energy. All calories are *not* equal. To achieve optimal health, you must not only count calories; you must consider the benefits each food provides.

Based on the healthiest eating habits worldwide, the Spa regime also conforms to the U.S. Dietary Guidelines and the latest findings of the American Cancer Society and the American Heart Association. It's no small coincidence that the low-fat, low-sodium, high-fiber diet that we favor is also the best kind of preventive medicine.

More than a temporary trend, spa cooking shows signs of achieving a permanent place in our national diet. As you look around today, even those dining in *haute cuisine* restaurants are eating less sauce, less salt, less sugar, and less red meat. And they are eating more fish, more grills, more salads, and more vegetables. At Jack's, the low-calorie Spa dishes have always won praise from discriminating diners, and within the next two decades I believe every restaurant menu will include spa food. It is happening already in New York and Los

My philosophy of healthful eating is simple, based on old-fashioned common sense. The four key principles are:

QUALITY   Use only the freshest, best, and most beautiful ingredients, emphasizing low-calorie, low-fat foods, whole grains, fresh fruits, and vegetables.

QUANTITY   Less is more; practice portion control and moderation in everything. (There are few limitations on the kinds of food you can use in Spa cooking, if you use just a small amount. You can occasionally indulge in high-calorie foods if you just have a taste—literally.)

VARIETY   Employ a broad range of foods from all categories. A broader selection of dishes will make your adjustment to new eating habits enjoyable and interesting.

VISUALS   Present food with an artistic eye; set the stage for a pleasurable experience involving all the senses by laying the table with care, arranging fragrant flowers.

Angeles and Dallas, because everywhere you go, across the United States and around the world, people are concerned with their health.

Hand in hand with this heightened nutritional awareness goes the knowledge that a regular program of exercise contributes as much to fitness as does a healthy diet. You could lose weight strictly by limiting your calorie intake, but it would not necessarily help you live longer. Nor will diet alone tone your body. Because not only does exercise help take off pounds; it replaces fat with muscle, burns calories far more efficiently than fat, gives your body a firmer, more youthful appearance, and improves your cardiovascular health. Exercise also increases the flow of oxygen to the brain, cuts your appetite, regulates blood sugar levels, speeds up your metabolism for several hours afterward, and reduces stress—as damaging to your well-being as a bad diet. At the Spa we encourage our guests to be more active, both during their visit and after their stay.

Olivia de Havilland, for example, had to gain twenty-two pounds for her starring role in *The Queen Mother*. After filming, she came to the Spa for a week, stayed for a month, and eventually lost twenty-seven pounds. What she especially loved was the early-morning mountain hike, and now she regularly begins her day with a long walk. We constantly hear stories of guests who change their lives in small but ultimately large ways after experiencing the remarkable health benefits and sense of well-being that result from a vist to the Spa.

When I first mentioned to my father my plans for building the Spa, he pointed out that it was inevitable, given my background. Now my family are frequent visitors here. On occasion, if my father feels he is getting a cold, he may come to have a series of herbal wraps, which help to eliminate toxins, and after a few days he goes home feeling rejuvenated. It may, of course, just be an excuse to visit.

Planning the Spa at the Sonoma Mission Inn, I envisioned an emotional and physical retreat. I wanted to create a total environment—insular and self-centered—that would permit guests to focus on themselves, their needs, and their desires. It is a great luxury to be able to leave the daily responsibilities of work and family behind, to do something positive for your health. But it is also enormously beneficial. Guests find that when they feel good, that sensation enhances all aspects of life on their return home.

We hope we can convey the supportive environment and peaceful surrounding of the Spa in this book, and motivate our readers to treat themselves to a spa program at home. If the menus and recipes that follow inspire you to modify your eating and exercising habits after completing the program, all the better. Because, beneficial as a stay at the Spa is, a week is still only a week—and the lessons of the Spa are really a way of life.

—E.J.S.

# THE SPA
# PROGRAM

## 850
### CALORIE
### MENUS

## 850
CALORIE MENUS

At the Spa, we obtain our remarkable results through a carefully devised program of exercise combined with a dietary regimen based on 850-calorie menus. By following the recipes in this section—all presented exactly as they are served at the Spa—you can enjoy the same Spa food and reap the same health benefits as our guests, at your convenience. Use the recipes for one dish, one meal, one day, or one week; the more closely you follow our Spa regime, the greater your losses—and gains—will be.

We wish that every single reader could spend at least a day at the Spa to absorb the rhythm and feeling of well-being and luxury that comes from focusing entirely on health, beauty, and self. Here's what it's like:

You will arrive at the Sonoma Mission Inn on a Sunday afternoon. Walking from the Inn down a path edged by sweet-scented lavender and lilac, passing the turquoise exercise pool, you will come upon the Spa itself. Outside, its pink stucco facade is a rounded structure, simple, clean, and unassuming. The moment you push open the massive oak doors, however, you are in another world—an ultramodern fitness facility. The serendipitous discovery is both exciting and energizing. Entering the Spanish-inspired atrium, you hear the soothing sounds of rushing water from the central rose marble fountain. Forty-foot rounded ceilings, skylights, and glass walls create an airy, open feeling. And "the orderly rows of columns" says designer Charles Swerz, "were designed to create a calm atmosphere and aid mental discipline." Off the atrium to the left are the spacious exercise studio and gyms where you will work out. To the right is the bathhouse, where, afterwards, you may indulge in a sybaritic sauna, steam, or whirlpool, water treatment or massage.

On your first afternoon you are interviewed about dietary concerns, then measured and weighed hydrostatically. This is the most accurate way to determine the percent of lean weight (muscle and bone) versus fat, and so the best way to calculate your ideal weight.

Sunday evening is your first taste of Spa cuisine, as you are introduced to your compatriots over a leisurely meal of grilled swordfish in the elegant Privée room, designed by Perry Wolfman. There, pink stucco, accented by mauve cotton and chintz, French doors with balloon shades, and a fireplace create a warm, inviting atmosphere. The seductive setting makes dining a sensual pleasure, whether by candlelight at night or with the French doors open to the morning sunlight.

Your first Spa supper begins with a fresh spinach salad with enoki mushrooms. The main course is a meaty swordfish steak accompanied by tiny new potatoes, green beans, and tangy pineapple-mustard purée. For dessert, a luscious shortcake of fresh peaches, topped with a dollop of whipped cream. The grand total—only 379 calories.

Monday is an optional 500-calorie cleansing day, or juice fast, to help rid the body of toxins. The menu consists of six high-energy fruit and vegetable drinks, each formulated to have a specific beneficial effect. For instance, the early-morning Orange-Strawberry Frappe is an instant energy booster loaded with vitamin C; the evening Blueberry-Nectarine Smoothie, fortified with bananas, replaces potassium lost during the day.

And what happens between meals? A typical day begins with a 5:45 wake-up call and a cup of herbal tea, followed by the morning hike among the redwoods in scenic Jack London State Park. Breakfast is from 7:45 to 8:30. The morning is devoted to body conditioning: 8:30 warm-ups, 9:00 aerobics, 10:00 slimnastics for toning muscles. At 11:00 you might have a facial, then at 12:00 work out on the exercise equipment in one of our two fully equipped gyms.

At 1:00 your efforts are rewarded with a sunny poolside lunch followed by pool exercise at 2:00. The rest of the afternoon is for relaxing with hydrotherapy, herbal wrap, or massage. Hydrotherapy is a stimulating underwater massage that applies soothing pressure with 30 bubbling jets and a hand-held hose. It increases circulation, stimulates heart and lungs, and aids in the elimination of toxins. The herbal wrap relaxes muscles, draws out toxins, and softens the skin. At 5:00 you might attend a class in stress management or yoga. "Cocktails" or a wine tasting begins at 6:45, followed by dinner and a lecture on a topic such as nutrition.

After five days at the Spa, eating meals just like the ones in this section, the average loss for women is 4 to 5 pounds and 7 inches overall. We recommend that women adhere to the 850-calorie regimen for five days for rapid weight loss, then go on the maintenance plan of 1,200 calories in the next section for continued, but slower, weight loss. Men need more calories than women, so at the Spa we give them 950 calories, serving them a hearty juice in the morning, such as the Nutty Almond-Pineapple Blend, and 1½ portions of the lunch entrée. After the first week, we suggest a 1,400-calorie diet for men. Naturally, consult your physician before beginning any new diet.

Take the time to do something good for yourself. Plan a special Spa week at home and follow the recipes in this chapter for five consecutive days. Start off or wind up your Spa week with a cleansing day. For best results, simultaneously engage in an exercise routine (see Exercise: A Way of Life, page 156). Then, for positive reinforcement, reward yourself with something relaxing like a massage or a facial. Remember, we believe you need not suffer to be beautiful and fit, so be good to yourself when Spa-ing at home.

**N O T E :** Because calorie counting is a somewhat imprecise science, the caloric values of these dishes should be considered approximate. Therefore, although some of the menus that follow may fall slightly short of (or exceed) 850 calories, they are close to the target range of 850 calories per day.

# CLEANSING DAY

7:45 A.M.
Pineapple-Lime Purée

10:50 A.M.
Carrot-Apple Concoction

1:00 P.M.
Vegetable Broth

3:50 P.M.
California Citrus Juice

7:00 P.M.
Papaya-Banana Smoothie

8:00 P.M.
Cucumber-Mint Frappe

The cleansing day is a wonderful re-juvenative treatment, particularly high in vitamins and minerals that are easily absorbed. Despite the small portions, the diet gives you enough energy to get from one meal to the next. At the Spa, where our guests burn a lot of calories during the day, we rarely hear complaints about hunger, although everyone is extremely enthusiastic about breakfast the next morning.

We think of cleansing days—on which meals consist of four small glasses of fresh fruit juices, one soup, a special evening drink, and two small servings of nuts—as a restorative. The juices act as body cleansers, flushing out toxins and giving your digestive system a rest. Another benefit comes from the high alkaline content of the juices, which counteracts any buildup of acids, creating a healing environ-ment in which your body's balance can be renewed.

A cleansing day is a good way to begin a diet, because it prepares your body for maximum weight loss; and it is equally effective as part of a mainte-nance program once you have reached your target weight. In fact, we recommend that you have a cleansing day once a week, preferably on the same day each week—perhaps Mon-day, after a self-indulgent weekend. Use only the freshest fruits and vege-tables, make sure they are well chilled, and prepare the juices just before drinking them in order to receive their full nutritional value.

NOTE: The cleansing diet is *not* rec-ommended for anyone with diabetes or hypoglycemia, or anyone who is under a doctor's care. Again, always consult your physician before starting this or any other diet.

## MENU

### BREAKFAST/7:45
PINEAPPLE-LIME PURÉE

### JUICE BREAK/10:50
CARROT-APPLE CONCOCTION

### LUNCH/1:00
VEGETABLE BROTH
MIXED NUTS AND SEEDS

### JUICE BREAK/3:50
CALIFORNIA CITRUS JUICE

### DINNER/7:00
PAPAYA-BANANA SMOOTHIE
MIXED NUTS AND SEEDS

### NIGHTCAP/8:00
CUCUMBER-MINT FRAPPE

## PINEAPPLE-LIME PURÉE

### 64
CALORIES PER SERVING

A delicious tropical blend full of potassium and papain, a digestive en-zyme. A reminder: be sure the pineapple is cold before you peel and core it.

½ pineapple, peeled and cored
Juice of 1 lime

Cut the pineapple into medium-size chunks. Purée with the lime juice in a blender or food processor. Serve at once in chilled goblets.

MAKES FOUR ½-CUP SERVINGS

## CARROT-APPLE CONCOCTION

### 80
CALORIES PER SERVING

The fresh taste of apples in this deli-cious drink mellows the intense flavor of the carrots.

3 medium red Delicious apples, unpeeled
6 medium carrots, cleaned

Put the carrots and apples through an electric juicer. (The ma-chine will strain out cores and seeds.) Serve at once in chilled goblets.

MAKES FOUR ½-CUP SERVINGS

## VEGETABLE BROTH

### 49
CALORIES PER SERVING

A good pick-me-up drink, even on days when you're not fasting.

*1 quart Vegetable Broth (page 163)*
*4 teaspoons finely chopped scallions*

Heat the broth to a boil and pour into heated mugs or soup bowls. Top with scallions. Serve the broth with small bowls of nuts and seeds.

**MAKES FOUR 1-CUP SERVINGS**


## MIXED NUTS AND SEEDS

### 50
CALORIES PER SERVING

*4 tablespoons unblanched almonds*
*4 tablespoons raw sunflower seeds*

Mix the almonds and sunflower seeds. Divide half the mixture among four small bowls and serve with the vegetable broth, reserving the remainder for dinner.

**MAKES EIGHT 1-TABLESPOON SERVINGS**


## CALIFORNIA CITRUS JUICE

### 53
CALORIES PER SERVING

Lots of vitamins A and C here!

*2 large pink grapefruit*
*Juice of 1 lemon*

Squeeze the grapefruit and lemon by hand or with a citrus juicer. Stir thoroughly and serve in iced glasses.

**MAKES FOUR ½-CUP SERVINGS**


## PAPAYA-BANANA SMOOTHIE

### 100
CALORIES PER SERVING

Rich in the digestive enzyme papain, papayas are generally available year round. If they are not at their peak of ripeness, plan to buy them a few days in advance and let them ripen to their luscious best on a sunny windowsill.

*2 papayas*
*½ banana*
*4 ice cubes, crushed (½ cup crushed ice)*

Peel and seed the papayas and cut into chunks. Peel and slice the banana. Purée the papaya and banana in a blender or food processor, add the ice, and continue to purée until smooth. Pour into chilled glasses and serve at once with small bowls of nuts and seeds.

**MAKES FOUR ½-CUP SERVINGS**


## CUCUMBER-MINT FRAPPE

### 26
CALORIES PER SERVING

Cucumber and mint are a classic combination in Middle Eastern cooking. Cucumber is a natural diuretic.

*3 cucumbers*
*2 teaspoons honey*
*12 large fresh mint leaves*
*4 ice cubes, crushed*

Peel the cucumbers, cut in half lengthwise, and scrape out the seeds with a spoon. Cut into chunks and purée in a blender or food processor with the honey and eight of the mint leaves. Add the ice and continue to purée until smooth. Pour into chilled goblets and garnish each with a mint leaf.

**MAKES FOUR ½-CUP SERVINGS**

CLEANSING
DAY

7:45 A.M.
Orange-Strawberry
Frappe

10:50 A.M.
Nutty Almond-Pineapple
Blend

1:00 P.M.
Gazpacho

3:50 P.M.
Grapefruit-Tangerine
Juice

7:00 P.M.
Blueberry-Nectarine
Smoothie

8:00 P.M.
Sweet Sesame
Nightcap

## M E N U

### B R E A K F A S T / 7 : 4 5

O R A N G E - S T R A W B E R R Y
F R A P P E

### J U I C E  B R E A K / 1 0 : 5 0

N U T T Y  A L M O N D -
P I N E A P P L E  B L E N D

### L U N C H / 1 : 0 0

G A Z P A C H O
M I X E D  N U T S  A N D  S E E D S

### J U I C E  B R E A K / 3 : 5 0

G R A P E F R U I T -
T A N G E R I N E  J U I C E

### D I N N E R / 7 : 0 0

B L U E B E R R Y - N E C T A R I N E
S M O O T H I E
M I X E D  N U T S  A N D  S E E D S

### N I G H T C A P / 8 : 0 0

S W E E T  S E S A M E
N I G H T C A P

# ORANGE-STRAWBERRY FRAPPE

## 65
### CALORIES PER SERVING

Make sure the oranges and strawberries are cold before you begin to make the juice. This is rich in vitamins A and C.

8 juice oranges, peeled
6 large strawberries, hulled

Juice the oranges on an electric juicer. (For a richer, more filling drink, squeeze the oranges by hand and remove the seeds with a spoon.) Purée with the strawberries in a blender. Serve at once in chilled goblets.

**MAKES FOUR ½-CUP SERVINGS**

# NUTTY ALMOND-PINEAPPLE BLEND

## 85
### CALORIES PER SERVING

Toasted almond butter provides protein as well as calcium, phosphorus, and potassium, and imparts a deep, nutty flavor to this blend. It is available at health food stores, or make your own with toasted almonds in a food processor. Bananas are rich in potassium, so frozen bananas are always handy for quick drinks and desserts. To freeze them, peel the bananas, rub with lemon juice, and cover immediately with plastic wrap to prevent discoloration.

2 tablespoons toasted almond butter
1 cup crushed ice
1 frozen banana, cut into chunks
¼ pineapple, peeled, cored, and cut into chunks

Put all the ingredients in a blender or food processor and purée. Serve at once in chilled goblets.

**MAKES FOUR ½-CUP SERVINGS**

# GAZPACHO

## 47
### CALORIES PER SERVING

There are as many versions of this Spanish national soup as there are households in Spain. Ours, flavored with fresh herbs, supplies plenty of vitamin A and potassium and is a good alternative to Cold Spiced Tomato Soup (page 114). It also makes a light low-calorie portable summer lunch. Or serve it as the soup course for any meal that does not already include tomatoes.

¼ onion
⅓ cucumber, peeled and seeded
¼ green pepper
⅓ garlic clove
1 teaspoon minced fresh coriander (cilantro)
1½ cups canned imported plum tomatoes, drained, or 5 ripe tomatoes, unpeeled, seeded and chopped
1 (6-ounce) can tomato juice
1 tablespoon extra-virgin olive oil
1 tablespoon red wine vinegar
1 teaspoon lemon juice
Pinch of vegetable seasoning
Dash of Tabasco sauce

4  *inner celery stalks with leaves*
1  *tablespoon minced chives*
1  *tablespoon minced fresh basil or parsley*

Place all the ingredients except celery, chives, and basil in a blender or food processor and purée until very smooth. Chill and serve, along with whole celery stalks, in cold soup bowls topped with herbs. Serve with small bowls of almonds and sunflower seeds.

**MAKES FOUR 1-CUP SERVINGS**


# MIXED NUTS AND SEEDS

## 50

CALORIES PER SERVING

Seeds and nuts supply the protein, oils, and minerals you need when fasting, and, of course, even a 1-tablespoon serving gives you something to chew on.

4  *tablespoons unblanched almonds*
4  *tablespoons raw sunflower seeds*

Mix the almonds and sunflower seeds. Divide half the mixture among four small bowls and serve with gazpacho, reserving the remainder for dinner.

**MAKES EIGHT 1-TABLESPOON SERVINGS**


# GRAPEFRUIT-TANGERINE JUICE

## 42

CALORIES PER SERVING

This super citrus combination has a sweet-sour tanginess, and is a high-C source of energy. Chill the fruit before making the juice.

1  *grapefruit*
3  *tangerines*

Peel the fruits and juice on a hand or electric juicer. Blend. Serve in chilled goblets.

**MAKES FOUR ½-CUP SERVINGS**


# BLUEBERRY-NECTARINE SMOOTHIE

## 93

CALORIES PER SERVING

The frozen bananas, which are also used in two other cleansing day recipes, replace potassium lost during the day, as do the blueberries and nectarines, which also provide vitamin C.

12  *ounces blueberries (fresh or frozen without sugar)*
2  *medium nectarines, pitted and cubed*
2  *small frozen bananas, sliced*
2  *tablespoons brewer's yeast*

Purée all of the ingredients in a blender. Serve in chilled goblets with small bowls of the reserved mixed nuts and seeds.

**MAKES FOUR ½-CUP SERVINGS**


# SWEET SESAME NIGHTCAP

## 68

CALORIES PER SERVING

Served as a nightcap, our rich sesame butter and fruit blend topped with a dash of nutmeg will lull you happily to sleep. The sesame butter is full of protein, niacin, calcium, iron, phosphorus, and potassium, and the dates add potassium, calcium, and iron.

2  *tablespoons sesame butter (tahini)*
½  *cup apple juice*
½  *frozen banana, cut into chunks*
2  *pitted dates*
5  *ice cubes*
   *Dash of freshly grated nutmeg*

Purée all of the ingredients except the nutmeg in a blender. Pour into chilled goblets and sprinkle with nutmeg.

**MAKES FOUR ½-CUP SERVINGS**

# DAY 1

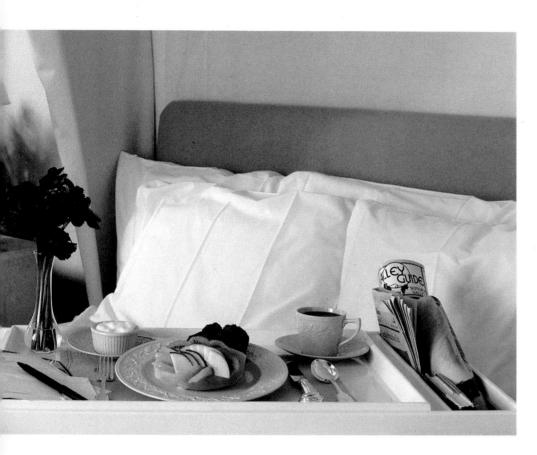

## BREAKFAST
### 251
#### CALORIES

PAPAYA FILLED WITH
FRESH SUMMER FRUITS

SPICY CINNAMON-APPLE
MUFFINS WITH YOGURT

HERBAL TEA OR
DECAFFEINATED COFFEE

# LUNCH
## 180
### CALORIES

SPA CHEF'S SALAD

SWEET CINNAMON-
ORANGE SORBET

HERBAL TEA OR
DECAFFEINATED COFFEE

# PAPAYA FILLED WITH FRESH SUMMER FRUITS

## 112
### CALORIES PER SERVING

Ripe, velvety papayas filled with luscious fruit look so appetizing and taste so good that you may think the nutritional benefits are incidental. In fact, this breakfast has plenty of vitamins A and C, as well as the protein-digesting enzyme papain.

- 2 ripe papayas
- 2 kiwi fruit
- 1 navel orange
- 1 nectarine or peach
- 1 red Delicious apple
- 2 teaspoons fresh lime juice

With a vegetable peeler, remove the skin from the papayas. Cut them in half lengthwise and scrape out the seeds with a spoon. Peel the kiwis and cut each into 8 thin rounds. Arrange 4 rounds in each papaya half.

Peel the orange, separate into segments, and put them in a mixing bowl. Cut the nectarine in half, remove the pit, cut into 1/4-inch dice, and add to the orange segments. Core the apple, cut into 1/4-inch dice, and add to the mixing bowl.

Sprinkle the lime juice over the cut fruit and toss quickly to keep the apple from turning brown. Arrange one quarter of the fruits in each papaya half and serve.

**SERVES 4**

# SPICY CINNAMON- APPLE MUFFINS WITH YOGURT

## 139
### CALORIES PER SERVING

Nutmeg, cinnamon, and zesty orange rind spice these moist, delectable muffins. Prepare the batter, then bake the muffins while you cut up the fruit for the papaya boats, or make the muffins the night before and reheat in the morning—the aroma from the oven is irresistible. You may want to make two batches at once and freeze some for another time. Each contains 123 calories.

- 1 1/2 cups stone-ground whole-wheat flour
- 1/2 cup bran flakes (miller's bran)
- 3/4 teaspoon baking soda
- 1/4 teaspoon freshly grated nutmeg
- 1/8 teaspoon ground cinnamon
- 2 teaspoons grated orange rind
- 1/2 cup peeled chopped apple
- 1/4 cup raisins
- 1/4 cup chopped walnuts
  Juice of 1/2 orange
- 1 cup buttermilk
- 1 egg, lightly beaten
- 1/4 cup blackstrap molasses
- 1 tablespoon cold-pressed vegetable oil

- 1/2 cup plain low-fat yogurt

Preheat the oven to 350°F. Lightly butter 1-cup muffin forms, dust lightly with whole-wheat flour, then shake out the excess.

In a mixing bowl, combine the flour, bran, baking soda, nutmeg, and cinnamon. Stir in the orange rind, apple, raisins, and walnuts.

Combine the remaining ingredients except the yogurt in another bowl, then add to the dry mixture and stir quickly until blended; do not overmix. Fill the muffin tins two-thirds full and bake for 25 minutes.

Serve the muffins hot for breakfast, passing the yogurt separately in a small bowl. Let the remaining muffins cool on racks. For convenience, these can be wrapped individually in foil and frozen for 2 to 4 months.

**MAKES 12 MUFFINS**

## SPA CHEF'S SALAD

### 160

CALORIES PER SERVING

This is a casual salad that can be made and served quickly, without an elaborate presentation. At the Spa we use as many seasonal greens as there are at the market, for a medley of colors, textures, and flavors. Use tender dandelion leaves, Swiss chard, arugula, chicory, or escarole—whatever is freshest. Until you become accustomed to our generous salad portions this may seem like a lot of lettuce, but once the damaged and wilted leaves are discarded, you'll have a salad of manageable size. And remember, it's served as an entrée, not just a side dish, and provides enough nutrition and energy to keep you going until dinnertime.

- ½ head Boston lettuce
- ½ head romaine lettuce
- ½ head red leaf lettuce
- 1 bunch watercress, coarse stems removed
- 2 heads Belgian endive, coarsely chopped
- 2 hard-cooked eggs, sliced
- 4 scallions, thinly sliced
- 12 mushrooms, thinly sliced
- 12 cherry tomatoes
- 8 radishes, thinly sliced
- 1 red Delicious apple, skin on, cored, and cut into ½-inch cubes
- ¼ small avocado, peeled, pitted, and thinly sliced
- ¼ cup Spa Vinaigrette made with walnut oil

Wash the greens, pat dry, and tear into bite-size pieces. Wash and dry the watercress and leave whole. Combine all the ingredients in a large bowl and toss lightly to distribute dressing evenly. Divide among the plates and serve.

**SERVES 4**

## SPA VINAIGRETTE

### 25

CALORIES PER TABLESPOON

Like any vinaigrette, our basic dressing can be varied to suit the greens or the season, the other ingredients on hand, and, of course, your taste. In summer, add fresh basil, tarragon, savory, or oregano. Add chopped or pressed garlic (judiciously) or a drop or two of hot sauce for more piquancy. For a variation, you might wish to substitute cold-pressed walnut oil for a strong, distinctive flavor or fruity extra-virgin olive oil, and blend with a simple red wine or champagne vinegar. This recipe, which makes more than enough for 4 servings, will keep for a week in the refrigerator if it is tightly covered. Plan to make it a few days ahead; as it ages the flavors blend together and are enhanced.

- 2 tablespoons cold-pressed safflower oil
- 2 tablespoons rice wine vinegar
- 2 tablespoons sparkling mineral water
- 1½ tablespoons fresh lime juice
- 1 tablespoon grainy mustard (Pommery or Moutarde de Meaux)
- 2 tablespoons minced shallots
- 1 tablespoon chopped fresh chives
- 8 grinds white pepper
  Vegetable seasoning to taste

Put all the ingredients in a bowl and whisk to blend. Store in the refrigerator in a tightly covered container.

**MAKES ABOUT ¾ CUP**

## SWEET CINNAMON-ORANGE SORBET

### 20

CALORIES PER SERVING

Spicy and sweet with a hint of almond, cinnamon-orange sorbet is simple to prepare, and best made the night before.

- 2 orange-spice herbal tea bags
- 2 sweet almond herbal tea bags
- 1 cinnamon stick
- 1½ cups boiling water
- 1 cup fresh orange juice
- 1 teaspoon grated orange rind
- ½ teaspoon barley malt sweetener

### GARNISH

- 4 knotted strips of orange rind

Put the tea bags and cinnamon stick in a bowl and pour the boiling water over them. Allow the tea to infuse until it is very strong, about 5 minutes. Remove and discard the tea bags and cinnamon. Stir in the remaining ingredients and let the tea cool.

If you have an electric or hand-powered ice cream maker, follow the manufacturer's instructions for making sherbet. To make the sorbet in your freezer, put the bowl in the freezer and leave it until the tea is frozen solid, about 2 to 3 hours. Remove from the freezer and break the tea into large chunks with a fork. Transfer the chunks to a food processor and process with the metal blade until uniformly textured. Divide among 4 dessert dishes or return the sorbet to the bowl and replace in the freezer for at least 30 minutes. Serve topped with the knotted orange rind.

**SERVES 4**

# DAY 1

## DINNER

### 382
CALORIES

SPINACH SALAD WITH
ENOKI MUSHROOMS

GRILLED SWORDFISH WITH
GREEN BEANS AND NEW
POTATOES

GOLDEN PINEAPPLE–
POMMERY MUSTARD PURÉE

FRESH PEACH SHORTCAKE
À LA CRÈME

HERBAL TEA OR
DECAFFEINATED COFFEE

## SPINACH SALAD WITH ENOKI MUSHROOMS

### 59
#### CALORIES PER SERVING

A spicier and more exotic version of the classic spinach salad, ours features the delicate enoki mushroom set off by the sharper flavors of red pepper and onion, all topped with our garlicky herb dressing. The enoki mushrooms are grown in California and sold fresh, in plastic pouches, at many Oriental groceries as well as greengrocers. At the Spa, we use local unwaxed cucumbers, which are washed and then sliced with the skins. If only waxed cucumbers are available, peel them first. Without dressing, the salad contains 32 calories per serving.

½ pound young tender spinach leaves, washed and patted dry with a towel, stems removed
1 large cucumber
⅓ package enoki mushrooms, root ends trimmed
1 red bell pepper, stemmed, seeded, and cut into ¼-inch dice
½ cup minced red onion

½ recipe Fresh Herb and Garlic Dressing

Divide the spinach leaves among four salad plates. Cut the cucumber lengthwise into thin slices, pat dry with paper towels, and set aside for about 5 minutes. Roll up the cucumber slices and "plant" 5 or 6 mushroom stems in one end of each roll. Arrange the rolls over the spinach leaves, sprinkle with the diced red pepper and minced onion, sprinkle with dressing, and serve.

**SERVES 4**

## FRESH HERB AND GARLIC DRESSING

### 20
#### CALORIES PER TABLESPOON

Very popular among guests is our special spicy salad sauce, which derives its heady aroma and flavor from lots of fresh herbs, garlic, and Tabasco sauce. If you like garlic and herbs, you can splurge by adding them freely, as they have almost no calories. Prepare the dressing a few hours or, better still, a few days before serving, to allow time for the flavors to blend and mellow. Tightly covered, it may be stored for up to a week in the refrigerator.

½ cup water
2¼ teaspoons arrowroot mixed with 2¼ teaspoons cold water
4 teaspoons extra-virgin olive oil
2½ teaspoons fresh lime juice
2½ teaspoons red wine vinegar
⅛ teaspoon Tabasco sauce
Small pinch of vegetable seasoning
½ garlic clove, minced
1 tablespoon chopped fresh basil
1½ teaspoons chopped fresh parsley
1½ teaspoons chopped chives

Bring the water to a boil in a small saucepan, then whisk in the arrowroot mixture, which will instantly thicken the water. Remove from the heat, pour into a small bowl, and let cool. Stir in the remaining ingredients.

**MAKES ABOUT ¾ CUP**

## GRILLED SWORDFISH WITH GREEN BEANS AND NEW POTATOES

### 185
#### CALORIES PER SERVING

Meaty swordfish steaks are complemented by the tangy pineapple-mustard purée. Perfect *al dente* beans and new potatoes complete this satisfying main course, which can be prepared in less than 30 minutes.

4 small red-skinned new potatoes, scrubbed
1 pound young tender green beans, ends trimmed
1 pound swordfish steak (about 1 inch thick)

**GARNISH**
4 lemon wedges
Parsley sprigs

**TO PREPARE THE POTATOES:** Put them in a saucepan and add cold water to cover by 1 inch. Bring to a rolling boil, lower the flame, and cook at a rapid simmer for 18 to 20 minutes, or until fork-tender.

**TO PREPARE THE GREEN BEANS:** Fill a bowl with cold water. Bring 1 quart of water to a boil in a saucepan, add the green beans, and cook for 2 to 3 minutes. Drain and plunge into the cold water to stop the cooking and preserve the color, then drain again.

**TO PREPARE THE SWORDFISH:** Preheat the broiler. Broil the swordfish 6 inches from the flame for 5 minutes on each side. Check to see that the fish does not dry out.

To serve, cut the swordfish into 4 equal portions. Place each on a heated dinner plate and arrange the drained potatoes and green beans around them. (If the potatoes and green beans were ready well before the swordfish, bring another pot of water to a boil and, using a strainer, dip the vegetables into the boiling water for 30 seconds to reheat.) Garnish with lemon wedges and parsley and serve with a portion of pineapple-mustard purée on each plate.

SERVES 4

# GOLDEN PINEAPPLE–POMMERY MUSTARD PURÉE

## 17
### CALORIES PER SERVING

This sweet and tangy relish turns simple fare into a sumptuous meal. Juicy, ripe pineapple is puréed and then spiked with grainy mustard. What could be simpler? Once you've made it, you'll want to serve this relish with broiled or roasted chicken and other firm-fleshed seafood, such as broiled shrimps. Use a good quality whole-grain mustard, preferably Pommery or Moutarde de Meaux, imported from France in handsome crocks.

*3/4 cup fresh ripe pineapple chunks, well drained*
*1 tablespoon whole-grain mustard*

Purée the pineapple in a blender. Just before serving, stir in the mustard.

SERVES 4

# FRESH PEACH SHORTCAKE À LA CRÈME

## 121
### CALORIES PER SERVING

Our Peach Shortcake looks too opulent to be part of a low-calorie regimen: fresh peaches, little génoise cakes—and, to top it off, whipped cream! The génoises, it is true, are 90 calories each, but peaches have very few calories, about 20 per serving. And the cream? It is really our Spa Cream: sweetened nonfat skim milk, whipped in an immersion blender.

*2 ripe peaches*
*4 Spa Génoises (page 95) made without lemon peel and vanilla*
*1 recipe Spa Cream*

Cut an X in the tops of the peaches (to make them easier to peel) and plunge them into a pot of boiling water for 5 seconds. With a slotted spoon, transfer them immediately to a bowl of cold water and leave for 5 minutes. Dry the peaches, slip off the skins, cut them in half, and remove the pits. Cut each half into 4 or 5 wedges. Arrange the wedges and the génoises on dessert plates.
Make the Spa Cream and divide among the plates, spooning it over and around the peaches and génoises, and serve at once.

SERVES 4

# SPA CREAM

## 11
### CALORIES PER 1/4 CUP

No one who tastes this delicious whipped topping will believe it contains only 3 calories per tablespoon! In fact, it is sweetened nonfat skim milk whipped in an immersion blender (see "Equipment," page 165). We use it in many of our desserts, folded into a creamy mousse, as a topping for little génoises, or to dress up a simple bowl of fruit.
There are a few things to remember when you make the cream: the milk *must* be nonfat or it will not whip at all. The colder the milk, the higher and fluffier the peaks will be. Chill the beaker and the milk in the freezer for 30 minutes to an hour before whipping it. If it is not used within 10 minutes, the cream will return to a liquid state, so make the cream at the last minute.

*1/2 cup very cold nonfat skim milk*
*1/4 teaspoon barley malt sweetener*
*1/4 teaspoon vanilla extract*

Put the ingredients in the beaker of an immersion blender. Insert the whipping nozzle on the blender shaft, put it in the beaker, and turn on the motor. In a minute or two, you will have a surprisingly large amount of whipped milk. In texture and flavor it is lighter and more delicate than whipped heavy cream, but very satisfying. Serve immediately.

MAKES ABOUT 1 CUP

# DAY 2

# BREAKFAST
## 217
### CALORIES

AN EGG TO YOUR TASTE
WITH FRESH FRUIT

PEANUT-SESAME BUTTER
ON WHOLE-GRAIN TOAST

HERBAL TEA OR
DECAFFEINATED COFFEE

# LUNCH
## 269
### CALORIES

MINNESOTA WILD RICE
SALAD

CAROB-MAPLE MOUSSE

HERBAL TEA OR
DECAFFEINATED COFFEE

## AN EGG TO YOUR TASTE WITH FRESH FRUIT

### 109
CALORIES PER SERVING

Eggs are one of nature's most perfect sources of protein and the ideal way to start the day for sustained energy release. At the Spa we use fertile eggs (see page 164), but fresh regular eggs are perfectly acceptable.

The favorite breakfast food worldwide, eggs can be prepared in a thousand ways. However, when counting calories, the simpler the better. At the Spa we serve eggs baked in a ceramic ramekin lightly greased with unsalted butter. But for variety, you can certainly substitute soft-boiled or plain poached eggs (and save about 15 calories per serving). Any way you choose to cook them, egg whites should be firm and yolks runny.

### GARNISH
    2  apricots, split and pitted
    4  strawberries, hulled

    4  eggs
    1  scant teaspoon unsalted butter
       (for baked eggs)
    1  teaspoon vinegar (for poached
       eggs)

Before you cook the eggs, prepare the garnish by filling each apricot half with a strawberry and placing one on each serving plate.

**TO PREPARE BAKED EGGS:** Preheat the oven to 325°F. Very lightly butter the bottoms of 4 small ramekins, break an egg into each, place the ramekins on a baking sheet, and bake until the eggs are done, about 5 to 6 minutes.

**TO PREPARE SOFT-BOILED EGGS:** Put the eggs in a saucepan with cold water to cover. Place the pan over high heat and set a timer for 6 minutes. Bring to a boil, lower the heat, and simmer until the timer rings. When the eggs are cooked, pour out the boiling water and set the pot under cold running water for about 30 seconds, just long enough to cool them so they can be handled. Put the eggs in egg cups and cut off the tops with a serrated knife.

**TO PREPARE POACHED EGGS:** Add enough water to a saucepan to cover the eggs, add the vinegar (to help the whites coagulate), and bring to a simmer. One at a time, break the eggs into a saucer and slide them into the simmering water. Poach for about 4 minutes, or until the whites are set and the yolks are runny. Have a bowl of hot water ready. When the eggs are cooked, remove then with a slotted spoon, and dip the spoon and egg briefly into the hot water to rinse off the vinegar. Place the spoon on several layers of paper towels or a kitchen towel, to absorb some of the water. Slip each egg onto a dish.

However you cook the eggs, place the bowls or ramekins on the serving plates and serve at once.

**SERVES 4**

## PEANUT-SESAME BUTTER ON WHOLE-GRAIN TOAST

### 108
CALORIES PER SERVING

Sweetened with honey and spiced with cinnamon, this creamy breakfast spread is high in protein and in flavor. Use unsalted, unsweetened peanut butter, readily found in health-food stores, or make your own peanut butter in a food processor. It will keep in the refrigerator for up to a week. The spread is 30 calories per ½ tablespoon.

    6  tablespoons unsalted smooth
       peanut butter
    4  tablespoons soft tofu
    4  teaspoons sesame butter (tahini)
    4  tablespoons honey
       Pinch of ground cinnamon

    4  slices Grandma's Whole-Wheat
       Bread (page 82) or other whole-
       grain bread, toasted

Place all the spread ingredients in a small bowl and mash with a fork until smooth. Spread ½ tablespoon on each toasted bread slice and serve.

**SERVES 4**

# MINNESOTA WILD RICE SALAD

## 205
CALORIES PER SERVING

Originally created for the Spa, this spectacular salad has become one of the most popular dishes on the regular lunch menu at the Sonoma Mission Inn. Its star-shaped presentation certainly makes it one of the prettiest. Long white endive leaves fan out from a healthful heart of crunchy wild rice, creamy tofu, and red, white, and green vegetables. The interplay of textures and colors, and the luxurious walnut oil vinaigrette, will make it an instant success with your guests as well. If you love herbs, here is a chance to indulge yourself by adding more fresh tarragon and chives. The best wild rice comes from Minnesota, which is why we specify it. When planning, note that the wild rice preparation must begin the night before.

2⅔ cups raw wild rice
  1 teaspoon chopped fresh tarragon or ½ teaspoon dried
  1 garlic clove
  6 ounces firm tofu
  ¼ cup chopped chives
  2 tablespoons chopped Italian parsley
  1 small red onion, minced
  ½ red or green pepper, minced
  ½ cup Spa Vinaigrette (page 23) made with walnut oil
 10 cherry tomatoes
  2 large carrots
  2 large zucchini
 20 endive spears

The night before you serve the salad, cover the wild rice in cold water to cover and soak in the refrigerator until morning. Drain the wild rice and put it in a large kettle. Cover with 2 quarts of cold water and add the tarragon and garlic. Bring to a boil and cook until tender but not mushy, about 15 to 20 minutes. (Start testing the wild rice after 15 minutes.) Do not allow the grains to "pop." When done, drain the wild rice, remove the garlic, and let cool in a large mixing bowl.

Cut the tofu into small bite-size pieces and add to the cooled wild rice, together with the chives, parsley, onion, and pepper. Pour on the vinaigrette, toss gently to mix, and let stand at room temperature for 2 hours.

Just before serving, cut the cherry tomatoes in half. Shred the carrots and zucchini on a mandoline or with the fine shredder of a food processor.

Arrange 5 spears of endive in a star shape over two thirds of each serving plate. Spoon the wild rice–tofu mixture over the bottom of the leaves and mound the carrots and zucchini around the base of the rice, leaving the endive tips exposed. Place half a cherry tomato in each endive spear and serve.

SERVES 4

# CAROB-MAPLE MOUSSE

## 64
CALORIES PER SERVING

This thick mousse, flavored with pure Vermont maple syrup, brown sugar, and carob, should satisfy any sweet tooth. Be sure to use roasted carob (not raw), which can be bought in health-food stores.

  3 tablespoons roasted carob
1½ tablespoons pure maple syrup
1½ teaspoons brown sugar
  ⅛ teaspoon barley malt sweetener
  3 tablespoons water
  1 tablespoon nonfat skim milk
  ½ recipe Spa Cream (page 27) made with ¼ teaspoon vanilla extract and without sweetener

### GARNISH
  1 teaspoon unsweetened shredded coconut

Put all the mousse ingredients except the Spa Cream in a metal bowl and place over simmering water. Cook slowly for 3 minutes, remove from the heat, and let cool in the refrigerator. The mousse can be made ahead to this point. Immediately before serving, make the Spa Cream. Fold the cream into the mousse, using a rubber spatula. Spoon the mousse into 4 well-chilled dessert cups or glass goblets, top each with shredded coconut, and serve immediately.

SERVES 4

# DAY 2

## DINNER
### 364
CALORIES

CHILLED CALIFORNIA
STRAWBERRY SOUP

FILLET OF VEAL WITH
SHIITAKE MUSHROOMS

YELLOW SQUASH WITH
SHALLOT BUTTER

MANDARIN ORANGE
SORBET

HERBAL TEA OR
DECAFFEINATED COFFEE

# CHILLED CALIFORNIA STRAWBERRY SOUP

## 39
CALORIES PER SERVING

Our local California strawberries and crisp apples make this sweet soup a special starter for any occasion. Or, for a variation, serve it as a dessert course. The pretty pink color will brighten any party table. Slice the strawberries for the garnish in a fan shape for an elegant presentation.

Naturally, homemade apple juice made with an electric juicer is preferred, but you may substitute the unsweetened store-bought kind if necessary. It is critical to chill all ingredients for at least an hour before whipping up this frothy first course.

    1   cup strawberries, washed and
        hulled
    ½   cup apple juice
    ¼   cup nonfat skim milk

GARNISH
    4   strawberries

Put the strawberries, apple juice, and skim milk in the container of a blender and purée. Pour into chilled cups or glass goblets and garnish each with a perfect strawberry.

SERVES 4

# FILLET OF VEAL WITH SHIITAKE MUSHROOMS

## 285
CALORIES PER SERVING

Meaty wild mushrooms are a connoisseur's choice to complement veal. For a more exotic dish, use as many different wild mushrooms as you can find—chanterelles, morels, porcini, golden oak, or oyster mushrooms, to name only a few. Fall is the height of the wild mushroom season, but they are available fresh or dried year round at better greengrocers and gourmet shops. With its rich sauce, this luxurious dish is perfect for entertaining and will stand up to your best Cabernet, so pull out all the stops.

    1    cup Rich Veal Stock (page 162)
    1½   tablespoons arrowroot mixed with
         1½ tablespoons cold veal stock
    4    (4-ounce) veal fillets, cut
         from the loin
    2    teaspoons unsalted butter
    16   large fresh shiitake mushrooms,
         stems removed, sliced
         Vegetable seasoning to taste
    1    bunch watercress, large stems
         removed

If you will be broiling the veal fillets, preheat the broiler.

In a small saucepan, bring the veal stock to a boil and whisk in the arrowroot mixture, which will instantly thicken the stock. Reduce the heat and simmer for 5 minutes. Strain the sauce into a bowl and keep warm over a pan of hot water.

Broil the veal fillets 5 inches from the flame for 3 to 4 minutes on each side, or until they are just cooked.

In a large sauté pan, melt the butter over medium heat, add the mushrooms, and toss for 2 to 3 minutes. Remove from the heat, transfer

the mushrooms to a bowl, add vegetable seasoning, and keep warm. Scrape the pan juices into the bowl of sauce and stir.

To serve, place a fillet in the center of each warmed dinner plate. Ladle one quarter of the sauce over each fillet, then spoon the mushrooms over the top.

Arrange the cooked squash on one side of the veal and the watercress on the other. Serve at once.

NOTE: If you prefer to pan fry the fillets, set a nonstick frying pan over high heat, brush the surface very lightly with oil, and fry the veal for about 3 minutes on each side, or until cooked to your taste.

SERVES 4

# YELLOW SQUASH WITH SHALLOT BUTTER

## 23
CALORIES PER SERVING

This simple dish is a sophisticated marriage of flavors and textures—pale slices of yellow squash perfumed with shallots that have been lightly sautéed in butter. Serve it with the veal fillet, as we do for this meal, or with roasted or broiled chicken. At the Spa, we cook vegetables the French way, in lots of rapidly boiling water, but you may find it easier to steam the squash. Either way, cook it quickly and carefully only until al dente.

1 teaspoon unsalted butter
2 tablespoons minced shallots
2 large yellow squash or zucchini,
  scrubbed, ends removed, and
  sliced 1/8 inch thick

Melt the butter in a nonstick frying pan over low heat. Add the shallots and cook for 2 to 3 minutes, stirring occasionally.

Add the squash to a large pot of rapidly boiling water, or place it in a steamer basket over boiling water. Cook for about 1 minute, or until crisp-tender. If the squash was boiled, drain it. Add the squash to the pan with the shallots and toss lightly.

SERVES 4

# MANDARIN ORANGE SORBET

## 17

### CALORIES PER SERVING

Fresh fruit sorbets are a special feature of our Spa cuisine. The secret ingredient in this dessert is freshly made carrot juice. You can make your own in a juicer or buy it in a health food store (and drink what is left over for a beauty bonus of vitamin A). Try to find a source for organically grown carrots. Their flavor is incomparably fresher and more vivid, and they are nutritionally superior to supermarket carrots. If fresh mandarin oranges are not available, use tangerines, clementines, or navel oranges.

2/3 cup water
1 tablespoon date sugar
1/8 teaspoon barley malt sweetener
1 tablespoon grated orange rind
2 cups fresh mandarin orange juice
1/3 cup fresh carrot juice
1 tablespoon fresh lemon juice

GARNISH
4 sprigs mint or 1 large orange

To make a Spa simple syrup, put the water, date sugar, and barley malt sweetener in a small saucepan and bring to a boil. Pour into a bowl and let cool. Stir in the rind and juices.

If you have an electric or hand-powered ice cream freezer, follow the manufacturer's instructions for making sherbet. To make the sorbet in your freezer, put the bowl in the freezer and leave it until the liquid has frozen solid, 2 to 3 hours. Remove from the freezer and with a fork break up the sorbet into large chunks. Transfer the chunks to a food processor and process with the metal blade until smooth and creamy. Return to the bowl and freeze for at least 30 mintues more.

To serve, place four 3-ounce (6-tablespoon) scoops of sorbet on chilled dessert plates and top with mint sprigs. To serve the sorbet as shown in the photo, use a sharp paring knife to remove the skin from the orange in one continuous strip, starting at the top and going all the way to the bottom. Cut the strip into 4 long strips and wrap around the sorbet.

MAKES ABOUT 3 CUPS

VARIATIONS: Using this same simple procedure, there is an endless variety of fruits and juices that can be transformed into a refreshing dessert. Or, simply frozen into fruit pops, purées make a cooling, vitamin-rich snack. If the fruit is at its peak of ripeness, it will need no additional flavorings or sweeteners, although a pinch of barley malt sweetener may be added if the fruit looks riper than it actually turns out to be.

The best fruits for simple sorbets are very ripe cantaloupes or other melons, mangoes, raspberries, strawberries, blueberries, and blackberries.

Melons and mangoes should be peeled, seeded, and diced. Berries should be picked over, hulled, and cleaned. Purée the fruit in the food processor. Raspberry, strawberry, and blackberry purée should be pushed through a fine sieve to remove the seeds. And, with the addition of a simple syrup like the one used here, refreshing sorbets can be made from lemons, limes, grapefruit, or oranges.

The amount of fruit you purée is up to you. Calculate the calories by measuring the fruit and consulting a calorie chart. At the Spa we calculate a 3-ounce scoop (6 tablespoons) of Cantaloupe Sorbet at 60 calories. When the sorbet is frozen, if you do not plan to use it immediately, transfer to a freezer container and label the container with the name of the fruit, the number of portions, and the calories per portion.

Pineapple Lime Sorbet is another tempting sorbet variation. Substituting a tangy mixture of pineapple purée and fresh lime juice for the juice makes for a refreshingly different sorbet that's especially cooling with our spicy Chicken Tostada lunch. Simply combine 1 1/4 cups ripe pineapple purée with 3/4 cup fresh lime or lemon juice, 2 teaspoons grated lime or lemon rind, 1/4 cup water, and 1/8 teaspoon barley malt sweetener. Prepare as above, and serve in chilled dessert glasses, garnished with slices of lime (see photo, page 37). Makes four 49-calorie servings.

# DAY 3

## BREAKFAST
### 199
CALORIES

SUMMER FRUIT BASKET

CINNAMON-ORANGE
POPPY SEED BREAD

HONEYED APPLE BUTTER

HERBAL TEA OR
DECAFFEINATED COFFEE

# L U N C H
## 295
### CALORIES

CHICKEN CORIANDER
TOSTADA WITH REFRIED BEANS

PIQUANT TOMATO SALSA

PINEAPPLE-LIME SORBET

HERBAL TEA OR
DECAFFEINATED COFFEE

## SUMMER FRUIT BASKET

### 64
CALORIES PER SERVING

The essence of summer, this colorful combination of mouth-watering fruits looks good enough to serve to guests at any meal. It is rich in vitamins A and C and high in postassium, so its beauty is more than skin deep. We prepare each fruit separately, then mix them and serve immediately so there is no loss of nutritional values and the distinctive flavor of each fruit is preserved.

- 1 cup blackberries
- 1 cup raspberries or strawberries
- 1 mango
- 1 papaya

Pick over the blackberries. If you are using strawberries, hull them and cut in half. Peel and seed the mango and papaya and cut each into ½-inch dice.

When you are ready to serve, mix the fruits and serve in chilled bowls.

**SERVES 4**

## CINNAMON-ORANGE POPPY SEED BREAD

### 124
CALORIES PER ½-INCH SLICE

A Spa staple, this poppy seed bread has a subtle hint of sweet oranges and spicy cinnamon. The sesame seeds and poppy seeds give it a wonderful wake-up crunch. It received such rave reviews from guests that we now use it for croutons in Jack's Caesar Salad and for stuffing our holiday turkey. You might also serve it at teatime, cut into small squares and spread with Honeyed Peanut-Sesame Butter.

- 1¼ cups stone-ground whole-wheat flour
- ½ cup raw sesame seeds
- 2 tablespoons noninstant nonfat dry milk
- 2 tablespoons poppy seeds
- 1½ tablespoons baking powder
- ½ teaspoon salt
- ¼ teaspoon ground cinnamon
- 2 eggs, lightly beaten
- ¼ cup honey
- ¼ cup fresh orange juice
- 2 tablespoons unsalted butter, melted and cooled
- 2 tablespoons almond oil or other cold-pressed vegetable oil

Preheat the oven to 350°F.

In a medium-size mixing bowl, combine the flour, sesame seeds, dry milk, poppy seeds, baking powder, salt, and cinnamon. Stir until well blended.

Mix the remaining ingredients in a small bowl and stir into the dry mixture. Mix just until blended. Spoon the batter into an 8-inch nonstick loaf pan (or one that has been lightly buttered and dusted with whole-wheat flour) and bake for 35 to 40 minutes, or until a toothpick inserted into the center comes out clean. Set the pan on a wire rack and let stand for 15 minutes. Turn the loaf out onto the rack and let cool for 10 minutes before slicing.

**MAKES ONE 8-INCH LOAF**

## HONEYED APPLE BUTTER

### 11
CALORIES PER TABLESPOON

A sweet gloss to any of our Spa breakfast breads, this spicy butter works especially well with the Cinnamon-Orange Poppy Seed recipe—with cinnamon as a common denominator. You can put the Honeyed Apple Butter through a sieve for a smoother finish. Or, for more texture and a fruitier flavor, add ¼ teaspoon grated orange or lemon rind. You can also substitute a pinch of ground cloves and mace for the cinnamon and nutmeg. Quantities may be doubled and the butter stored tightly covered in the refrigerator for up to a week. Serve hot or cold.

- 1 small Golden Delicious apple
- 1 teaspoon unsalted butter
- 1 teaspoon honey
- ¼ teaspoon water
  Pinch of freshly grated nutmeg and ground cinnamon, mixed

Peel, core, and coarsely chop the apple. Put it in a small heavy-bottomed saucepan with the remaining ingredients, cover, and cook over low heat for 5 to 10 minutes, or until the apples are soft. Check occasionally to see that the apple is not sticking to the bottom. If it is, add another ¼ teaspoon of water and lower the heat. When the apple is cooked, put the mixture in a bowl and mash with a fork. (For larger amounts, the spread may be puréed in a blender.) Spread 1 tablespoon on a slice of the poppy seed bread.

**SERVES 4**

## CHICKEN CORIANDER TOSTADA WITH REFRIED BEANS

### 231
CALORIES PER SERVING

Chicken Tostada makes a lavish lunch with exciting contrasts in texture and color, served with a spicy tomato salsa. Its only seasonings are the fresh herbs; of course, it is the coriander that gives the dish its characteristic Mexican flavor. Coriander (also known as cilantro or Chinese parsley) is a green parsleylike herb with a distinctive, pungent flavor and a slightly sweet, lemony scent. It is used frequently in Mexican, Asian, and Middle Eastern cooking. Packaged corn tortillas can be found in the dairy or freezer departments of most supermarkets.

4  small boneless half chicken breasts, skin on (3 to 4 ounces each)
1/2  cup cooked pinto beans
1/4  cup minced red onion
1  garlic clove, mashed
1  tablespoon extra-virgin olive oil
4  corn tortillas
4  cups chopped green leaf lettuce
1/4  cup chopped chives mixed with 1/4 cup chopped fresh coriander
2  ounces Cheddar cheese, shredded

Piquant Tomato Salsa

GARNISH
1/2  red pepper, stemmed, seeded, and cut into julienne strips

Preheat the broiler.
Broil the chicken breasts for about 5 minutes on each side, or until cooked through but not dry. Leaving the broiler on, remove the chicken, cut off and discard the skin, and keep the breasts warm.

If you are using canned pinto beans, rinse off the salty canning liquid under running water and drain the beans. With a fork, mash 1/4 cup of the beans, then put them in a small saucepan with the remaining beans and the onion, garlic, and olive oil. Stir to blend the ingredients and heat gently.

To toast the tortillas, place them in a baking pan large enough to hold them in a single layer and bake until crisp, about 3 to 5 minutes. Remove from the oven and leave in the pan. Layer each tortilla as follows: one quarter of the beans, spread over the entire surface; one quarter of the chopped lettuce; a chicken breast; one quarter of the chopped herbs; and finally one quarter of the shredded cheese. Place the tostadas under the broiler just long enough to melt the cheese.

With a large spatula, transfer the tostadas to 4 serving plates, ladle 1/4 cup of salsa next to each, top with red pepper, and serve.

SERVES 4

## PIQUANT TOMATO SALSA

### 15
CALORIES PER 1/4 CUP

Salsa is a spicy seasoned sauce usually made with chili peppers, widely used in Mexican-American and Tex-Mex cookery. It is additionally used for dipping or as a condiment with main courses. This piquant version—low in calories and high in flavor—can also be served as a relish for broiled fish or chicken, as a pick-me-up for a platter of plain steamed vegetables, or even as a pasta sauce (if you add chopped basil instead of coriander).

Buy only the ripest, juiciest tomatoes, or use canned imported plum tomatoes. Make the sauce mild or wild, as you like it. Many greengrocers carry one or two kinds of fresh hot peppers. If you can't find jalapeños, buy at least two of whatever variety is available, then perform a pungency test by cutting off a small piece and tasting it (have a glass of water handy!). Use canned pickled jalapeños as a last resort, but be sure to rinse off the brine.

2  ripe, juicy tomatoes, peeled and seeded, or 1/2 cup imported canned plum tomatoes, drained
1/3  white Bermuda onion
1/3  green pepper
1/3  red pepper
1  medium jalapeño pepper (or to taste), minced
Juice of 1 lime
1  garlic clove, minced
1  teaspoon minced Italian parsley
2  tablespoons chopped fresh coriander
Vegetable seasoning to taste

Cut the tomatoes, onion, and green and red pepper into 1/4-inch dice. Put in a bowl, add the remaining ingredients, and stir to blend well. Let stand at room temperature for 2 hours to allow the flavors to blend.

MAKES ABOUT 1 CUP

## PINEAPPLE-LIME SORBET

### 49
CALORIES PER SERVING

See Variation, Page 35.

# DAY 3

# DINNER
## 360
### CALORIES

ASPARAGUS SPEARS WITH LEMON DRESSING

GRILLED SHRIMP AND VEGETABLES
WITH DILLED YOGURT SAUCE

BLUEBERRY MOUSSE

HERBAL TEA OR
DECAFFEINATED COFFEE

## ASPARAGUS SPEARS WITH LEMON DRESSING

### 65
CALORIES PER SERVING

This is an elegant and easy first course which can be prepared ahead for entertaining. Fresh asparagus tips are arranged on a bed of leaf lettuce, garnished with chopped egg and parsley and a splash of lemon dressing. Choose slender young asparagus spears (the stalks should not be woody or dry), cook them early in the day, and add the dressing just before serving. Rich in vitamins A and C, with only 3 calories per stalk, asparagus is the quintessential diet food.

25 slender asparagus spears
4 large romaine leaves

DRESSING
1½ tablespoons olive oil
1½ tablespoons fresh lemon juice
1 tablespoon water

GARNISH
8 thin julienne strips lemon rind

Cut off the asparagus about 2 to 2½ inches below the tips. (Reserve the asparagus bottoms for making a wonderful stock.) To cook, bring 3 quarts of water to a rapid boil, add the asparagus tips, and cook for about 5 minutes, or until the vegetable is crisp-tender. Taste a piece (the cook's bonus) to see if it is done to your liking. The tips may instead be steamed over boiling water for 3 to 4 minutes.

When done, immediately plunge the cooked asparagus into a large bowl of cold water and leave until cool. Drain the tips, pat dry with a towel, wrap in paper towels to keep crisp, and refrigerate.

To serve, place a romaine leaf on each salad plate and arrange 6 asparagus tips over each.

Combine the dressing ingredients in a cup, blending well with a fork, and drizzle 1 tablespoon over each serving. Decorate with the lemon rind strips.

SERVES 4

## GRILLED SHRIMP AND VEGETABLES WITH DILLED YOGURT SAUCE

### 249
CALORIES PER SERVING

These colorful shrimp kebabs, presented on a bed of brown rice and wild rice, are one of the most popular Spa dishes. Each kebab contains 219 calories, and two tablespoons of the sauce add only 30 more. We use bamboo skewers to hold the shrimps, red and green peppers, onions, and mushrooms in place while turning them over an outdoor fire, or under the broiler indoors. Easy to prepare and quick, this is an ideal party dish for summer entertaining outdoors, in your back yard or at the beach. When making this for guests, plan ahead: wild rice must be soaked the night before.

You can cook the brown rice and wild rice anytime during the day and, after they are mixed, reheat them in the top of the double boiler in minutes.

⅓ cup raw brown rice
3 tablespoons minced onion
  Vegetable seasoning to taste
⅓ cup raw wild rice, soaked overnight in cold water to cover
1 medium white Bermuda onion
½ medium red pepper
½ medium green pepper

1 pound large shrimps, shelled and deveined (12 to 16 shrimps)
8 mushrooms, stemmed
1 teaspoon cold-pressed vegetable oil

DILLED YOGURT SAUCE
½ cup Spa Mayonnaise
1 tablespoon chopped fresh dill

GARNISH
4 lemon wedges

Cook the brown rice and wild rice separately. To cook the brown rice, bring 1½ quarts of water to a rolling boil and add half the minced onion, a dash of vegetable seasoning, and the rice. Let the rice simmer until tender but not mushy, about 40 minutes.

Drain the wild rice and cook in 1½ quarts of boiling water with the remaining minced onion and vegetable seasoning to taste. The wild rice will be ready in 15 to 20 minutes. Begin to check for doneness after 15 minutes. When it is cooked, drain well and mix with the brown rice. Cover and keep warm, or reheat later in the top of a double boiler.

While the rice is cooking, cut the onion into eight 1-inch squares. (Reserve leftover onion for another dish.) Cut each half pepper into four 1-inch squares. Bring 2 quarts of water to a boil and blanch the onion and pepper for 30 seconds. Drain and refresh under cold running water. Cool and pat dry.

Preheat the broiler.

Thread each skewer as follows: shrimp, onion, shrimp, pepper, mushroom; repeat, using a piece of both red and green pepper on each skewer. Brush the shrimp and vegetables with the oil and broil 6 inches from the flame for 3 to 4 minutes on each side.

Combine the Spa Mayonnaise and chopped dill to make a sauce.

To serve, place a skewer on each heated dinner plate and add the brown rice and wild rice and a lemon wedge. Serve with a bowl of the Dilled Yogurt Sauce.

**SERVES 4**

# SPA MAYONNAISE

## 15

### CALORIES PER TABLESPOON

Our basic mayonnaise is very high in protein, very low in calories, and may be flavored to suit the occasion.

- ¼ cup soft tofu
- 1 tablespoon plain low-fat yogurt
- 1 hard-cooked egg
- 1 teaspoon lemon juice
- 1 tablespoon minced shallots
  Pinch of salt or vegetable seasoning
  Tabasco sauce to taste

Purée the tofu, yogurt, egg, and lemon juice in the bowl of a food processor or mash with a fork. Scrape into a small bowl, add the remaining ingredients, and let stand for at least an hour.

**MAKES ABOUT ½ CUP**

# BLUEBERRY MOUSSE

## 46

### CALORIES PER SERVING

A simple concoction of fresh blueberries, sweetened with honey and date, and whipped Spa Cream, this airy mousse is delightfully light. If you think you may be pressed for time or are having guests, the blueberry base can be made early in the day or even the night before and the Spa Cream added at the last minute.

If you can spare a few calories (just 15 or so per serving), peel a kiwi fruit, cut it into 8 thin rounds, and place 2 of them against opposite sides of each dessert bowl, projecting above the rim, before spooning the mousse into the bowls.

- 1 cup blueberries
- 2 teaspoons water
- 1 tablespoon honey
  Pinch of barley malt sweetener
- 1 pitted dried date
- 1 teaspoon arrowroot mixed with 1 tablespoon cold fresh orange juice
  Spa Cream (page 27), made with ⅓ cup of nonfat skim milk and without sweetener

### GARNISH
4 blueberries

Pick over the blueberries. Put them in a saucepan with the water, honey, barley malt sweetener, and date. Bring to a boil and cook for 1 minute. While the mixture is at the boil, whisk in the dissolved arrowroot, which acts as an instant thickener, and cook for 1 minute more. Pour into a blender and purée, then pass through a fine sieve. Place in a bowl and refrigerate until completely cold, about 1½ hours.

Make the Spa Cream just before serving. Reserve ¼ cup of the cream and carefully fold the rest into the cold blueberry mixture, using a rubber spatula.

Spoon the mousse into 4 chilled dessert bowls, top each with a tablespoon of cream and a blueberry, and serve at once.

**SERVES 4**

# DAY 4

## BREAKFAST
### 186
#### CALORIES

CHILLED GRAPEFRUIT
AND FRESH MINT COUPE

CHEWY CASHEW-DATE
BUTTER ON
WHOLE-GRAIN TOAST

HERBAL TEA OR
DECAFFEINATED COFFEE

## LUNCH
### 299
#### CALORIES

BIBB AND RED LEAF
LETTUCES VINAIGRETTE

HOT PASTA PRIMAVERA
WITH BASIL SAUCE

ICED CAPPUCCINO

## CHILLED GRAPEFRUIT AND FRESH MINT COUPE

### 50
CALORIES PER SERVING

A refreshing dash of crème de menthe added to the grapefruit makes this breakfast fruit cup a lively eye-opener. It tastes even better when the flavors have been allowed to blend overnight. If you make it just before serving, use chilled grapefruit.

    3  large grapefruit
    1  teaspoon green crème de menthe
    1  tablespoon chopped fresh mint

**GARNISH**
    4  mint sprigs

As you peel each grapefruit, hold it over a bowl to catch the juices. With a sharp knife, cut through the skin to remove the white membrane along with the peel. Section the grapefruit by cutting down to the core on either side of the inner membranes to free the segments, then dig out the seeds with the point of the knife. Put the segments in another bowl. Squeeze the rinds and membranes over the bowl of juice and discard them. Stir the crème de menthe and chopped mint into the juice and pour over the grapefruit segments. Cover tightly with plastic wrap and refrigerate.

To serve, divide the grapefruit sections and juice among 4 bowls and top each with a sprig of mint.

**SERVES 4**

## CHEWY CASHEW-DATE BUTTER ON WHOLE-GRAIN TOAST

### 136
CALORIES PER SERVING

Hearty and substantial, with nuggets of chewy dates throughout, this is another delicious breakfast spread. Cashew butter, which can be bought in health food stores, should be covered and refrigerated to keep from spoiling. This recipe will make about a cup of spread, which is 58 calories per tablespoon.

    4  slices Grandma's Whole-Wheat
       Bread (page 82) or other whole-
       grain bread
    ½  cup cashew butter
    8  pitted dried dates, finely chopped
    ¼  cup soft tofu

Toast the bread. Put the remaining ingredients in a bowl and mash well with a fork, or for larger quantities the butter may be prepared in a blender or food processor. Spread one tablespoon on each slice of toast and serve, refrigerating leftover spread.

**SERVES 4**

## BIBB AND RED LEAF LETTUCES VINAIGRETTE

### 63
CALORIES PER SERVING

To begin our classic Italian luncheon, we serve a summery salad lightly tossed with our Spa Vinaigrette. If you can't get Bibb lettuce, substitute Boston, or hydroponically grown lettuce. Instead of red leaf lettuce, ruby-red radicchio would also be beautiful. For the vinaigrette use a fruity extra-virgin Italian olive oil; the best comes from the Valley of Lucca in Tuscany.

    ½  head Bibb lettuce
    ¼  head red leaf lettuce
    4  radishes, sliced
    8  mushrooms, sliced
    4  cherry tomatoes
    ½  cup Spa Vinaigrette (page 23),
       made with extra-virgin olive oil

Wash the lettuces and pat dry. Tear each into bite-size pieces and put in a salad bowl. Add the radishes, mushrooms, tomatoes, and vinaigrette and toss gently to mix. Divide among 4 salad plates.

**SERVES 4**

# HOT PASTA PRIMAVERA WITH BASIL SAUCE

## 226
CALORIES PER SERVING

Spa guests love this dish, which is more primavera than pasta. The seeming abundance of pasta is really an illusion. Carrots and zucchini are cut to the size and shape of the pasta, cooked *al dente*, and then tossed with a fresh basil sauce. Added to only an ounce of pasta per serving, they create a splendid *trompe l'oeil* effect. Buy fresh or frozen whole-wheat egg pasta, or use dried imported whole-wheat pasta. With our pasta we use Asiago, an aged Italian cheese with a flavor similar to Parmesan but more mellow. Freshly grated Parmesan is just as delicious. The Spa Pesto and the Basil Sauce may be made well in advance of serving.

### BASIL SAUCE

- 2 teaspoons extra-virgin olive oil
- 1 tablespoon unsalted butter
- 3 tablespoons Spa Pesto (page 83)
- 3 tablespoons Chicken Stock (page 161)
- 1 cup low-fat skim milk
- 1 ½ tablespoons arrowroot mixed with 1 ½ tablespoons water
  Freshly ground white pepper to taste
  Vegetable seasoning to taste

- 2 carrots
- 2 small zucchini
- ¼ pound whole-wheat pasta
- 1 tablespoon unsalted butter
- 2 tablespoons minced shallots
- 12 mushrooms, sliced
- 1 tablespoon pine nuts
- 2 tablespoons Spa Pesto
- 4 cherry tomatoes
- ¼ cup freshly grated Asiago or Parmesan cheese

**TO PREPARE THE BASIL SAUCE:** Put the olive oil, butter, and pesto in a small heavy saucepan and cook gently over medium heat for 2 minutes; do not allow to brown. Add the stock and milk and bring to a boil over high heat. Add the arrowroot mixture, which will instantly thicken the sauce, and boil for 2 minutes. Add pepper and vegetable seasoning to taste. If you prepare the sauce a day ahead, transfer it to a small bowl, cover tightly with plastic wrap, and refrigerate. Otherwise, reserve the sauce in the pot and keep hot.

**TO PREPARE THE SALAD:** The carrots and zucchini should be cut up separately to the width and thickness of whatever pasta you have. An adjustable mandoline can easily be set to the proper measurements. However, a food processor can also be used, with very good results. If your pasta is fettuccine, use a knife to cut the vegetables to the width of the pasta, then slice them on the thin slicing blade; if you are using linguine, put the vegetables through the julienne blade; for spaghetti or vermicelli, use the fine shredder. (You might want to consider your shredding equipment before you buy the pasta.)

In a saucepan, bring 3 quarts of water to a rolling boil. Put the carrots in a strainer and dip them into the boiling water for 30 seconds. Lift out of the boiling water and immediately rinse under cold running water to stop the cooking. Drain and set aside with the raw zucchini. Add the pasta to the boiling water and cook until it is tender but still firm to the bite. Drain the pasta and rinse it under cold running water. Drain again and set aside.

Reheat the basil sauce, if necessary.

Melt the butter in a large sauté pan over medium heat, add the shallots, and cook for 1 minute. Stir in the mushrooms and pine nuts, cook for 1 minute, then add the carrots, zucchini, and pesto and cook, stirring, for 1 minute more. Add the basil sauce and pasta and toss for 15 seconds to reheat the pasta.

To serve, divide the pasta and vegetables among 4 heated dinner plates. Top each portion with a cherry tomato and sprinkle with 1 tablespoon of cheese. Serve at once.

**SERVES 4**

# ICED CAPPUCCINO

## 10
CALORIES PER SERVING

Cinnamon and whipped Spa Cream transform cold coffee into a luxurious liquid dessert. If you are on a caffeine-free regimen, use decaffeinated espresso coffee, either freshly brewed or instant.

- 1 quart cold espresso, preferably freshly brewed
- ½ recipe of Spa Cream (page 27)

- 4 pinches of ground cinnamon
  Barley malt sweetener and honey to taste

Pour the coffee into tall chilled glasses. Whip the cream and spoon it over the coffee. Sprinkle with cinnamon, and serve at once. Serve the barley malt sweetener and honey separately.

**SERVES 4**

# DAY 4

## DINNER
### 355
CALORIES

COLD CUCUMBER SOUP WITH FRESH DILL

HALIBUT STEAMED IN LETTUCE LEAVES
WITH NEW POTATOES

BROILED TOMATOES WITH
GARLIC BUTTER

MANGO-CHAMPAGNE ICE CREAM SODA

HERBAL TEA OR
DECAFFEINATED COFFEE

## COLD CUCUMBER SOUP WITH FRESH DILL

### 76
CALORIES PER SERVING

This refreshing dill-flavored soup is easy to make ahead and ideal to have on hand for spur-of-the-moment summer entertaining. Its flavor will be greatly enhanced if you make it with a good homemade chicken stock. If you love dill, feel free to add more, since it is very low in calories.

 1 tablespoon unsalted butter
 ½ leek (white part only), washed, patted dry, and chopped
 ¼ medium onion, chopped
 2 cucumbers, peeled, seeded, and chopped
 1 quart Chicken Stock (page 161)
 ½ cup low-fat skim milk
   Freshly ground white pepper to taste
   Vegetable seasoning to taste
 1 tablespoon chopped fresh dill

### GARNISH

 ⅓ cucumber, seeded and cut in 4 rectangles, 2 x 1½ inches each
 4 sprigs fresh dill

In a 3-quart saucepan, melt the butter over medium heat, add the leek, onion, and cucumber, and sauté for 2 minutes. Add the stock and bring to a boil. Reduce the heat and simmer the vegetables, uncovered, for 20 minutes. Purée the soup in a food processor or blender in several batches (the hot liquid will increase in volume dramatically as it is puréed). Pour into a bowl, let cool to room temperature, and refrigerate until cold, about 1½ hours. The soup can be prepared ahead to this point.

To serve, stir in the skim milk, pepper, vegetable seasoning, and dill. Pour into chilled soup bowls and serve with cucumber rectangles and sprigs of dill.

SERVES 4

## HALIBUT STEAMED IN LETTUCE LEAVES WITH NEW POTATOES

### 180
CALORIES PER SERVING

Halibut fillets, wrapped in red leaf lettuce and steamed over fish stock, are served on a bed of aromatic vegetables and fresh herbs. If you make the halibut packages early in the day (using fish bought that morning), the dish can be completed in about 25 minutes. After the fish has been steamed, cool and freeze the stock for future use, its flavor now further enriched by the halibut juices.

 8 large leaves red leaf lettuce
 4 (4-ounce) halibut fillets
 2 tablespoons minced shallots
 4 small new red potatoes, unpeeled
 1 quart Fish Stock (page 160)
 1 tablespoon unsalted butter
 1 medium leek (white part only), washed, patted dry, and cut into julienne strips
 1 large celery stalk, cut into julienne strips
 1 carrot, peeled and cut into julienne strips
 ½ zucchini, cut into julienne strips
 ¼ cup water
 1 tablespoon each chopped fresh chives, parsley, basil, and tarragon

To prepare the halibut packages, have a bowl of ice water ready. Bring 3 quarts of water to a boil and blanch the lettuce leaves for 2 seconds. Immediately scoop up the leaves with a slotted spoon or wire strainer and plunge them into the ice water. Carefully spread the leaves on towels and pat dry.

For each package, overlap 2 lettuce leaves and place a piece of fish in the center. Sprinkle 1½ teaspoons of shallots over each fillet and wrap the lettuce around it, completely enclosing it. If the packages are made in advance, cover them tightly with plastic wrap and refrigerate.

About 25 minutes before serving, put the potatoes in a saucepan with cold water to cover, bring to a boil, reduce the heat, and cook at a fast simmer until they are fork-tender, about 15 to 20 minutes.

Pour the stock into a steamer and bring to a boil. Place the halibut packages in the top of the steamer, lower into the pot, and steam for 5 to 8 minutes.

Just before serving, melt the butter in a large sauté pan, add the leek, celery, carrot, and zucchini, and toss for 1 minute. Add the water and chopped herbs and bring to a boil, stirring and tossing to combine the ingredients. Remove from the heat and divide the vegetables and their juices among 4 heated dinner plates. Place the halibut over the vegetables. Drain and slice the potatoes and place 1 on each plate. Serve at once.

SERVES 4

# BROILED TOMATOES WITH GARLIC BUTTER

## 24
### CALORIES PER SERVING

Ripe tomatoes, quickly broiled, are a good accompaniment for the halibut. You may use basil instead of parsley if you serve the tomatoes with another entrée.

½ garlic clove, mashed in a garlic press
1 teaspoon chopped parsley
1 teaspoon unsalted butter, at room temperature
Freshly ground white pepper to taste
Vegetable seasoning to taste
2 ripe tomatoes, stemmed and cut in half

Preheat the broiler. Mix the garlic, parsley, butter, and seasonings into a paste and spread over the cut sides of the tomatoes. Broil for 3 to 5 minutes, or until the tops are golden brown.

SERVES 4

# MANGO-CHAMPAGNE ICE CREAM SODA

## 88
### CALORIES PER SERVING

This colorful dessert tastes even better than it looks. Take Honey-Vanilla Ice Cream, add fresh raspberry purée, ripe mango, and a few ounces of mineral water, and you have the ice cream soda of your dreams. Adding just a tablespoon of champagne makes it taste even more special. If you decide to forgo it, however, you'll save about 13 calories.

⅔ cup, packed, fresh raspberries or unsweetened frozen raspberries, thawed
Barley malt sweetener to taste
6 tablespoons Honey-Vanilla Ice Cream
1 ripe mango, peeled, seeded, and cut into 12 slices
1 (8-ounce) bottle Sonoma Mission Inn mineral water or other carbonated mineral water
¼ cup champagne (optional)

An hour or so before serving, chill 4 glass goblets in the freezer.
Purée the raspberries in a blender or food processor and strain through a fine sieve to remove the seeds; you should have about ½ cup of purée. Taste the raspberries; if they need sweetening, add a very small pinch of barley malt sweetener.
For each serving, put a 1½ tablespoon scoop of ice cream in a goblet. Spoon 2 tablespoons of raspberry purée over the ice cream and top with 3 mango slices. Pour 2 tablespoons of mineral water and 1 tablespoon of champagne over the fruit, and serve at once.

SERVES 4

# HONEY-VANILLA ICE CREAM

## 68
### CALORIES PER ¼ CUP

This super-satisfying dessert has the aroma of vanilla and the richness of honey—with a paucity of calories. It can be enjoyed by itself or served with a variety of fresh fruits and berries. Strawberries and blueberries would make a festive red, white, and blue dessert.

6 egg yolks
3 tablespoons honey
⅛ teaspoon vanilla extract
2 cups low-fat skim milk

Mix the egg yolks, honey, and vanilla extract in a bowl.
In the top of the double boiler, scald the milk. Stir 2 tablespoons of the milk into the egg mixture to warm it, then pour the eggs into the milk all at once, stirring constantly. Set the pot over simmering water and cook for 3 to 5 minutes, stirring, until the custard coats the back of a spoon. Remove from the heat and let cool. Using an electric or hand-powered ice cream maker, freeze the cooled custard. This recipe can be doubled or tripled and, tightly covered, will keep for months.

MAKES 2⅔ CUPS

# DAY 5

## BREAKFAST

### 197
CALORIES

CRUNCHY SPA GRANOLA
WITH STRAWBERRIES
AND MILK

HERBAL TEA OR
DECAFFEINATED COFFEE

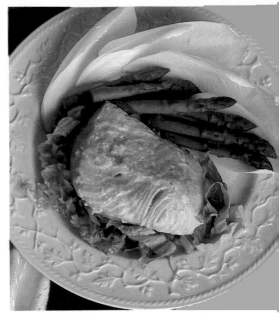

# LUNCH

## 278
### CALORIES

COLD POACHED SALMON
WITH ASPARAGUS TIPS
AND ENDIVE

SAFFRON MAYONNAISE

AUTUMN APPLE SORBET

HERBAL TEA OR
DECAFFEINATED COFFEE

# CRUNCHY SPA GRANOLA WITH STRAWBERRIES AND MILK

## 197
### CALORIES PER SERVING

This crunchy granola will test your willpower—you'll probably want seconds. Fortified with walnuts, almonds, wheat germ, sunflower and sesame seeds and flavored with cinnamon and honey, it's more like candy than cereal. Granola is also a wonderful topping for hot fruit cobblers, but use it sparingly; each tablespoon has 66 calories.

### SPA GRANOLA
- 1 cup rolled oats
- 1/3 cup chopped walnuts
- 1/3 cup whole unblanched almonds
- 2 tablespoons sunflower seeds
- 2 tablespoons sesame seeds
- 1 tablespoon raw wheat germ
  Pinch of ground cinnamon
- 1 tablespoon cold-pressed safflower oil or other cold-pressed vegetable oil
- 1 tablespoon honey

- 2 cups sliced strawberries
- 2 cups nonfat skim milk

**TO PREPARE THE GRANOLA:** Preheat the oven to 225°F.

Toss all the granola ingredients in a mixing bowl. Spread thinly on a baking sheet and bake for 20 to 25 minutes, stirring often so that the ingredients brown evenly. Watch carefully. When the granola is golden and the texture starts to become crunchy, remove and let cool. This recipe makes 2 cups of granola.

You may store granola in an airtight container, unrefrigerated, for up to 2 weeks.

To serve, place 1/2 cup of sliced strawberries in each bowl, top with 2 tablespoons of granola, and pour on 1/2 cup of milk.

### SERVES 4

**VARIATION:** Another delicious way to enjoy our granola is to serve it over yogurt. It tastes even better if the yogurt is fresh and homemade. Because yogurt is slightly more caloric than skim milk, which has only 45 calories per half cup, reduce the amount of yogurt to 1/3 cup to keep the calorie total at 197.

# HOMEMADE YOGURT

## 128
### CALORIES PER CUP

Homemade yogurt is not only delicious but surprisingly easy to make if you follow a few simple rules. First, if you are using plain commercial low-fat yogurt for a starter, use a high-quality brand and be sure it is free of stabilizers that kill the live bacteria. They may be listed as modified food starch, gelatin, guar gum, or locust bean gum. Next, make sure the dried skim milk you buy smells fresh; powdered milk standing on the store shelf too long can become rancid. The jars in which the yogurt is made and stored must be very clean and should have tightly fitting lids. Finally, in order to "set up," or thicken, the yogurt must sit undisturbed at a constant heat of from 106° to 116°F. A yogurt maker automatically ensures the correct temperature, but a heating pad turned to low will also do the trick, and a candy thermometer will enable you to monitor the temperature, especially the first few times you make it.

- 1 cup plain low-fat yogurt, homemade or commercial
- 1 cup nonfat liquid skim milk
- 3 cups noninstant nonfat dry milk
- 2 cups warm water (100° to 110°F.)

Put the yogurt in a bowl and slowly add the liquid skim milk, stirring until it is smooth. Stir in the dried milk a little at a time, then add the water, which should test "warm" on your wrist. Strain the mixture through a sieve to remove any lumps.

If you are using a commercial yogurt maker, pour the yogurt into the containers provided, cover tightly, and turn on the switch.

If you are using a heating pad, place it in a draft-free corner of the kitchen and turn the heat to low. Pour the yogurt into 4 clean 1-cup containers, cover them tightly, and place on the heating pad. Cover the jars with a warm damp towel.

Let the culture stand undisturbed for 6 to 10 hours. Check to see if the yogurt has set up by touching it lightly with your finger. If it resists even a little, it can be refrigerated. If you prefer a tangier, more acid yogurt, let it incubate a while longer. Do not shake or bump the containers until the yogurt is cool, or it might separate. Cover tightly and store in the refrigerator for up to 7 days.

**MAKES ABOUT 1 QUART**

## COLD POACHED SALMON WITH ASPARAGUS TIPS AND ENDIVE

### 178
#### CALORIES PER SERVING

This is a truly elegant lunch that looks elaborate but is very easy to arrange. Excellent for a formal luncheon where you want to enjoy your guests, it can be made ahead, so you have only to take the plates out of the refrigerator. Cold poached fish actually improves in flavor, so you could easily make it the night before. An alternative to the saffron-scented mayonnaise might be an herbed mayonnaise flavored with fresh chopped tarragon or dill. Serve it with lemon wedges and pass shakers of freshly ground white pepper and vegetable seasoning at the table.

    1   shallot, minced
    4   (2½-ounce) salmon fillets
    1   cup hot Fish Stock (page 160)
    24  slender asparagus spears
    1   quart thinly sliced green leaf
        lettuce
    24  endive spears (about 3 endives)

### GARNISH
    4   lemon wedges

Sprinkle the shallot over the bottom of a skillet just large enough to hold the salmon in a single layer. Place the salmon over the shallots and pour the hot stock into the pan. Cover with foil, seal tightly, and cook over medium heat for 5 to 8 minutes, or until the salmon is cooked but not dry. Check for doneness after 5 minutes. Drain the fish, cover, and refrigerate until cold. (Strain the remaining stock and reserve for another use.)

Bring 4 quarts of water to a rolling boil. Trim the asparagus into 3-inch spears (reserve the ends for stock) and boil them for 2 to 3 minutes. Drain the asparagus and plunge it into a bowl of ice water to stop the cooking and preserve the color. Drain, pat dry, and chill.

To serve, make a nest of lettuce on each plate and place salmon over it. Arrange the endive and asparagus around the salmon and serve, passing a bowl of Saffron Mayonnaise separately.

### SERVES 4

## SAFFRON MAYONNAISE

### 45
#### CALORIES PER SERVING

A subtle saffron flavor permeates this brilliant yellow sauce. Saffron must always be cooked to release its full aroma and taste. Here it is simmered with mushrooms, shallots, and vermouth, then strained and mixed with Spa Mayonnaise.

    ½   teaspoon saffron threads
    5   medium mushrooms, chopped
    1   tablespoon minced shallots
    1   tablespoon dry white vermouth
    ¼   cup water
    6   tablespoons Spa Mayonnaise (page
        43), made without shallots

Put all the ingredients except the mayonnaise in a small heavy saucepan. Over high heat, reduce the liquid to 1 tablespoon. Strain through a fine sieve, pressing on the vegetables to extract all the juices. Let cool, then stir into the mayonnaise.

### SERVES 4

## AUTUMN APPLE SORBET

### 55
#### CALORIES PER SERVING

For really fresh flavor, put red Delicious or McIntosh apples through an electric juicer. However, ½ teaspoon of grated orange or lemon rind will liven up bottled apple juice. In a pinch, you can buy freshly made apple juice from a health food store juice bar.

    2   cups unsweetened apple juice
    1   cup water
    ⅛   teaspoon barley malt sweetener

### GARNISH
    Thinly julienned lime rind

Combine all ingredients in a bowl.

If you have an electric or hand-powered ice cream freezer, follow the manufacturer's instructions for making sherbet. To make the sorbet in your freezer, place the bowl in the freezer and leave it until the liquid has frozen solid, 2 to 3 hours. Remove the sorbet from the freezer and break up into large chunks with a fork. Transfer the chunks to a food processor and process with the metal blade until smooth and creamy. Return to the bowl and freeze for at least 30 minutes more.

Serve in chilled goblets decorated with lime rind.

### SERVES 4

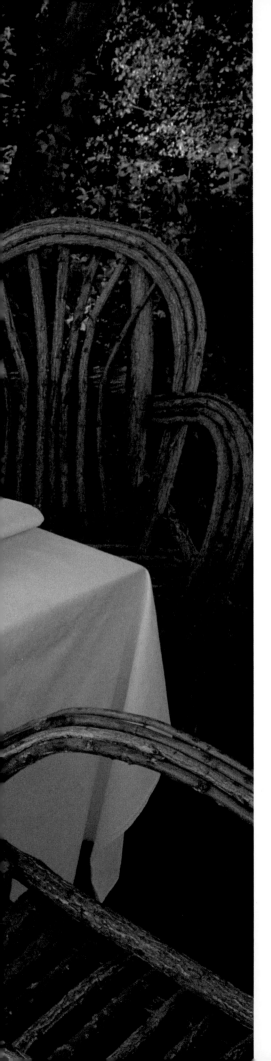

# DAY 5

# DINNER

## 356
### CALORIES

SPARKLING SONOMA
WHITE WINE SPRITZER

CHICKEN BREASTS
WITH WILD RICE

FRESH TOMATO SAUCE
WITH BASIL AND GARLIC

SAUTÉED ZUCCHINI

FRESH FRUITS ON A SKEWER
WITH RASPBERRY MOUSSE

HERBAL TEA OR
DECAFFEINATED COFFEE

## SPARKLING SONOMA WHITE WINE SPRITZER

### 65
CALORIES PER SERVING

Before lunch or dinner, introduce your friends to the low-calorie cocktail we serve at the Spa. You can use any dry white wine, such as an oaky Chardonnay, Chenin Blanc, or fruity Johannisberg Riesling.

2⅔ cups dry white wine
1⅓ cups sparkling mineral water

**GARNISH**
4 lemon or lime wedges

Put ice cubes in 4 chilled tall glasses or large goblets, add the wine and mineral water, and stir. Add lemon or lime wedges and serve.

**SERVES 4**

## CHICKEN BREASTS WITH WILD RICE

### 188
CALORIES PER SERVING

Straightforward, honest food—perfectly cooked—can be surprisingly satisfying. In fact, many French chefs, when queried about their favorite homecooked meal, said it was simple roast chicken! At the Spa, grilling imparts a special flavor, but if you don't have a home grill, a broiler is almost a good. This simple preparation is enlivened by our flavorful tomato sauce, made with lots of fresh basil and garlic. Note that the rice must soak overnight.

1½ cups wild rice, soaked overnight in cold water to cover

4 (4-ounce) boneless chicken breast halves, skin on

**TO PREPARE THE WILD RICE:** Bring 2 quarts of water to a rapid boil. Drain the wild rice and add to the pot. Let the wild rice simmer freely for 15 to 20 minutes, or until it is tender but still has a little crunch. Check for doneness after 15 minutes. Drain and keep warm, or cover the drained rice and reheat in the top of a double boiler just before serving.

**TO PREPARE THE CHICKEN:** Preheat the broiler.

Broil the chicken breasts for 3 to 4 minutes on each side. When they are done, remove the skin. (Cooking them with the skin on seals in flavor and keeps them from drying out.)

To serve, divide the wild rice among 4 heated dinner plates. Place a chicken breast on each plate. Spoon on a mound of tomato sauce and serve.

**SERVES 4**

## FRESH TOMATO SAUCE WITH BASIL AND GARLIC

### 28
CALORIES PER SERVING

When available, use the best organically grown fresh tomatoes you can find and freeze some of this sauce for the winter months. Good-quality imported canned plum tomatoes will serve you the rest of the year. This chunky sauce is delicious served with many grilled meats or fish. You can increase the basil and garlic to please your palate.

4 ripe tomatoes, or 1 cup imported canned plum tomatoes, drained
1 teaspoon olive oil
½ garlic clove, minced
1 tablespoon minced shallot
¼ cup water (for fresh tomatoes only)
1 tablespoon chopped fresh basil

To skin the fresh tomatoes, cut an X in the top of each, cut out the core, and drop into a pot of boiling water for 5 seconds. Immediately plunge the tomatoes into a bowl of cold water and strip off the skin. Cut the tomatoes into ¼-inch dice. If you are using canned tomatoes, simply dice them.

Heat the olive oil in a nonstick skillet, add the garlic and shallot, and sauté over low heat for 2 minutes. Add the fresh tomatoes and water (or the canned tomatoes) and simmer for 5 minutes. Keep warm, or reheat briefly just before serving, adding the basil at the last minute.

**SERVES 4**

# SAUTÉED ZUCCHINI

## 17
### CALORIES PER SERVING

The secret of our butter-flavored zucchini is that we use a nonstick skillet and sauté the vegetable with only a teaspoon of butter and two tablespoons of water, which evaporates as the squash cooks.

- 1  teaspoon unsalted butter
- 2  medium zucchini, cut into ¼-inch rounds
- 1  scallion, thinly sliced
- 2  tablespoons water

Melt the butter in a nonstick skillet, add the zucchini, scallion, and water, and sauté over medium heat for two minutes. Serve at once.

**SERVES 4**

# FRESH FRUITS ON A SKEWER WITH RASPBERRY MOUSSE

## 58
### CALORIES PER SERVING

Red raspberry purée mixed with our light whipped Spa Cream is the background for this colorful array of fresh fruits threaded on bamboo skewers. We alternate pieces of pineapple, kiwi, oranges, and strawberries for a dramatic presentation.

At the Spa, we buy cases of fresh raspberries during the summer, when they are plentiful, and make them into a purée, which we freeze and use thoughout the year to bring the taste of summer to our fall and winter menus. You can do the same (although perhaps not by the caseful). Alternatively, the whole raw raspberries, frozen without sugar or syrup, that are available at many supermarkets year round make a good purée.

**RASPBERRY MOUSSE**
- ⅔  cup, packed, fresh or frozen unsweetened raspberries, thawed
  Small pinch barley malt sweetener (optional)
- ½  recipe Spa Cream (page 27)

- 8  (1-inch) cubes fresh pineapple (about ⅔ cup)
- 1  kiwi fruit, peeled and cut into 8 pieces
- 8  navel orange segments
- 8  strawberries, hulled

Purée the raspberries in a blender or food processor, then pass through a fine sieve to strain out the seeds. You will have about ½ cup purée. Taste for sweetness. Set aside.

Make the Spa Cream and fold it into the raspberry purée.

Divide the mousse among 4 chilled dessert plates.

Thread 4 bamboo skewers with 2 pieces each of pineapple, kiwi, orange, and strawberry. Place a skewer of fruit on each plate, and serve at once.

**SERVES 4**

# THE SPA
# AT HOME

# 1,200
CALORIE
MENUS

## 1,200

This section is about bringing Spa-style eating habits to your everyday table, and modifying our menus to suit your personal goals and life-style. The kinds of fresh foods we use and the whole approach to preparing, presenting, and enjoying these meals are all part of a philosophy we hope you will adopt as your own.

Because the 850-calorie regimen should be followed only for a week at a time, the recipes and menus in this section provide a more generous 1,200-calories per day and can be used for either gradual weight loss or maintenance, depending on the individual. For the average person ideal weight is maintained by consuming somewhere between 1,200 and 1,500 calories. Twelve hundred calories will allow most women to eat very well and still maintain their target weight. Other women and the majority of men will experience gradual weight loss. Whatever your needs, you can adjust the size of the servings accordingly. Similarly, you can increase the portions of the 850-calorie menus to use them for maintenance instead of weight loss.

Of course, the exact number of calories required for maintaining a fixed weight varies with each individual, his or her metabolism, and their level of activity. Determining the number of calories required to maintain your ideal weight is difficult because it varies—even from day to day. The best method is probably trial and error. If you jog five miles one day, you will burn more calories than if you spend a sedentary Sunday perusing the newspapers, or a day sitting in the office. This is why diet and exercise must go hand in hand.

Keep in mind that if you are exercising regularly, replacing fat with muscle, your ideal weight will increase. One guest came to the Spa for a week and afterward complained that she had lost only 4 pounds—but she had also lost 8 inches overall! Body contour and muscle tone are as important as weight; your shape counts for more than the number on the scale.

If you are using these menus for gradual weight loss, it is important to be committed and consistent. Remember that weight comes off more quickly in the beginning, and the last few pounds as you near your goal are always the most difficult. But if you follow the Spa regime faithfully, at least 80 percent of the time, you should see some changes within two weeks. If not, consult your physician for other possible problems.

Organization is essential in preparing our Spa menus at home, just as it is when attempting to re-create any new cuisine. Read the meals for the week to come, perhaps on the weekend when you have more time. Note any time-consuming preparations, such as stocks (which can be made ahead and frozen), and plan accordingly. If you've taken advantage of seasonal produce, freezing fruit purées and tomato sauce, even better. Some breakfast items, like jams and muffins, can also be made ahead without losing their nutritional value; freezing foods does not significantly affect nutrients, although fresh is always better.

Adopt the French style of shopping for fresh fruits and vegetables every day. If you are pressed for time, discover reliable stores that deliver. Always have on hand plenty of mineral water, herbal teas, lemons, limes, and low-calorie crunchy snacks, such as celery, carrots, and radishes so that you are never hungry and tempted to resort to nonnutritional nibbles if you haven't yet weaned other members of your household away from such foods.

Organize your pantry: stock it with Spa staples (see the list on page 164) so that you don't run out of your favorite vinegar at the last moment and have to run to the store. Learn to scrutinize food labels with a wary eye and avoid sugar, salt, fats, and chemical additives. Beware of hidden calories lurking in sauces, salad dressings, fruit juices, and condiments, such as ketchup or mayonnaise. Buy a handy reference book and learn the nutritional values of your favorite foods—you may be pleasantly surprised.

Think of low-calorie "free foods" as "in." You can enjoy these in *almost* unlimited quantities: asparagus, bamboo shoots, bean sprouts, beet greens, broccoli, cabbage and Chinese cabbage, cauliflower, celery, cucumber, endive, eggplant, green beans, green peppers, lettuce, mushrooms, okra, radishes, romaine, scallions, spinach, sprouts, tomato, turnips, truffles, watercress, yellow squash, and zucchini. To add extra flavor to a favorite recipe you can make lavish use of "free" ingredients such as lemon, lime, all seasonings (other than salt), all spices and herbs, and extracts (up to 2 teaspoons a day). Salt substitutes are available in health-food stores.

On the "out" list are these foods: anything high in salt (which retains water), sugar, or fat, and everything with chemical additives. Other foods we frown on are fatty meats, such as bacon, ham, and sausages; fried foods; shortenings and margarine; and all soft drinks—including diet beverages.

Among beverages, sparkling and nonsparkling mineral waters, herbal teas, grain cereal beverages (for example, Cafix and Pero), and low-salt vegetable juices are "in."

Eat slowly. Don't rush. Even if you're in a hurry *never* eat standing up in front of the refrigerator. When possible, eat your meals with chopsticks; it will take longer to finish everything on your plate. Taking the time to prepare food properly and set the table gives you a chance to reflect on what you are about to put in your body, so there is less chance of impulse eating, nervous nibbling, and poor food choices.

When dining at home, try not to eat alone. If you do, make it a pleasurable ritual; all food tastes better and is more enjoyable when it is presented with style. Set a tantalizing table, light the candles, pour a glass of wine, and savor each mouthful. Lavish on yourself the same care and attention to detail as you would for a guest.

Following the menus we've designed here is a very important first step in bringing the principles we practice at the Spa into your own home—it means making a commitment to improving the quality of the food you prepare for yourself and others, as well as to obtaining your ideal weight.

# DAY 1

## BREAKFAST

### 334

CALORIES

POACHED EGGS AND
WHOLE-GRAIN TOAST
WITH JAM

HERBAL TEA OR
DECAFFEINATED COFFEE

# LUNCH
## 326
### CALORIES

HEARTY SPLIT PEA AND
BARLEY SOUP

ROMAINE, WATERCRESS,
AND ENDIVE SALAD

OLD-FASHIONED HOT
APPLE COBBLER

HERBAL TEA OR
DECAFFEINATED COFFEE

## POACHED EGGS AND WHOLE-GRAIN TOAST WITH JAM

### 334
CALORIES PER SERVING

This classic American breakfast can be made very quickly if you already have our bread and jam among your Spa staples. Eggs can even be poached ahead and reheated by a plunge into hot water for 30 seconds.

8 slices Grandma's Whole-Wheat Bread (page 82) or other whole-grain bread

1 quart water
1 tablespoon vinegar
8 eggs
  Paprika
1 large orange, cut into wedges
4 strawberries

8 tablespoons Homemade Strawberry Jam

Toast the bread and wrap it in a cloth napkin to keep warm while the eggs are poaching.

In a saucepan, bring the water and vinegar to a boil (the vinegar helps the egg whites coagulate), then lower the heat so that the water simmers. Break an egg into a saucer and slip it into the simmering water. Repeat for 3 more eggs, so that you poach 4 eggs at a time. Cook for about 2 minutes, or until the whites are firm but the yolks are still runny. Remove the eggs with a slotted spoon, dip briefly into a bowl of hot water to rinse off the vinegar, then hold a kitchen towel under the spoon to drain off the water. Place 2 eggs on each plate and sprinkle with paprika. Add a wedge of orange, a strawberry, 2 slices of toast, and 2 tablespoons of jam. Serve at once. If you prefer to serve this breakfast without the jam, place the eggs on the toast.

SERVES 4

## HOMEMADE STRAWBERRY JAM

### 9
CALORIES PER TABLESPOON

This jam looks ravishing and tastes wonderfully fresh. It makes a welcome gift. During the summer, when strawberries are plentiful, you can double or triple the recipe.

6 cups fresh strawberries or frozen unsweetened whole strawberries, thawed
2 tablespoons water
3 tablespoons honey
¼ teaspoon barley malt sweetener

Sterilize eight ½-cup canning jars by setting them upright in a tall pot and putting the lids in the pot. Add enough hot water to submerge the jars completely. Bring to a boil and boil for 15 minutes. Leave the jars in the hot water while you make the jam, removing and draining them just before the final addition of berries.

Wash and hull the strawberries. Cut 2 cups into small bite-size pieces and set aside. Cut the remaining 4 cups in half or into thirds and put them in a saucepan with the water. Bring to a boil, lower the heat to medium, and cook for 10 minutes, stirring constantly. Add the remaining berries, honey, and barley malt sweetener, and return to a boil. Boil for 1 minute only, then pour into the sterilized jars and seal at once with a tight lid. Store the jam in a cool pantry or cupboard or in the refrigerator for up to 2 months.

MAKES ABOUT 4 CUPS

# HEARTY SPLIT PEA AND BARLEY SOUP

## 145
### CALORIES PER SERVING

This is a homey, comforting soup, perfect for chilly winter days. Thick and flavorful, it will satisfy the hungriest appetite. Naturally, the richer the chicken stock, the better the soup. For convenience, it may be prepared a day or two in advance. The split peas and barley need no soaking before they are cooked.

1½ cups dried split peas
½ medium onion, coarsely chopped
½ carrot, cut into chunks
1 small celery stalk, cut into chunk
1 garlic clove
1½ quarts Chicken Stock (page 161)
½ cup pearl barley
    Freshly ground white pepper
    to taste
    Vegetable seasoning to taste

Put the peas, onion, carrot, celery, garlic, and stock in a 3-quart pot and bring to a boil. Lower the heat and simmer, uncovered, for 1 hour. Purée the soup in batches in a food processor or blender and return to the pot. Add the barley, bring to a boil, lower the heat, and simmer for 30 to 40 minutes, or until the barley i tender. Add the seasonings, ladle 1-cup servings into 4 heated soup bowls, and serve. Let the remaining soup cool and freeze for 1 to 2 months.

**MAKES 1½ QUARTS**

# ROMAINE, WATERCRESS, AND ENDIVE SALAD

## 38
### CALORIES PER SERVING

Plenty to chew on here! You can enhance the flavor by adding seasonal fresh herbs, or, if you're looking for ways to add calories and protein, sprinkle on some chopped walnuts to intensify the walnut oil vinaigrette.

½ head romaine
2 bunches watercress
24 endive spears (about 3 whole endives)
¼ cup Spa Vinaigrette (page 23) made with walnut oil

Wash the romaine, discarding damaged and wilted leaves, and pat dry. Remove the large stems from the watercress, wash the leaves, and dry them. Separate the endives into spears. Put the greens, endive, and dressing in a large bowl and toss, or arrange the greens on 4 salad plates and sprinkle each serving with 1 tablespoon of dressing.

**SERVES 4**

**VARIATION:** For a slightly more peppery flavor and elegant look, substitute an additional bunch of watercress for the lettuce and arrange the greens on individual plates. Sprinkle each portion with 2 tablespoons of dressing. This will serve up to eight people as a first course (see photo, page 136).

# OLD-FASHIONED HOT APPLE COBBLER

## 143
### CALORIES PER SERVING

Especially good in fall, when perfectly fresh apples are plentiful, this updated version of an American classic is almost as easy as serving plain sliced apples. But the honey-cinnamon flavoring is what makes it special—like eating the inside of an old-fashioned apple pie—and our Spa Granola adds a healthful crunchiness. For those who like their apples tart, omit the barley malt sweetener. If you are feeling extravagant enough to add 16 extra calories to each portion, top the cobblers with a tablespoon of Orange-Yogurt Sauce (page 90).

2 large red Delicious apples
    Juice of ½ lemon
⅛ teaspoon ground cinnamon
1 teaspoon honey
    Pinch of barley malt sweetener
1 tablespoon unsalted butter, melted
½ cup Spa Granola (page 54)

Preheat the oven to 350°F.
Peel and quarter the apples, cut out the seeds and core, then cut into ¼-inch wedges.
In a bowl, sprinkle the apples with the lemon juice, add all the remaining ingredients except the granola, and toss to mix. Divide the apples among 4 small individual baking dishes, or spread in a shallow 2-cup baking dish, and bake for 7 to 9 minutes. Sprinkle 2 tablespoons of granola over each cobbler and return to the oven for 3 minutes more. Serve piping hot.

**SERVES 4**

## DINNER
### 531
#### CALORIES

SEASONAL CRUDITÉS
CREAMY ROQUEFORT DIP

WHOLE BOILED LOBSTERS
WITH WILD RICE
AND LEMON BROCCOLI

CRANBERRY-RASPBERRY
MOUSSE

HERBAL TEA OR
DECAFFEINATED COFFEE

## SEASONAL CRUDITÉS WITH DIP

### 72
CALORIES PER SERVING

A multitude of low-calorie fresh vegetables—such as fennel, endive, and blanched snow peas—may be substituted for variety. Crunchy textures are most satisfying and provide a good contrast to our creamy Roquefort dip and even with a shared half cup of dip, crudités are still only 72 calories per serving. They are also ideal for a Spa cocktail party—or just to have at home for yourself for a healthful nibble. Prepare the raw vegetables close to serving time to preserve their nutrients.

    4  cauliflower florets
    4  small carrots
    2  celéry stalks
    4  scallions
    8  cherry tomatoes
    ½  cup Creamy Roquefort Dip

Have a bowl of cold water ready. In a saucepan, bring 1 quart of water to a boil, add the cauliflower, and blanch for 30 seconds. Drain and plunge into the cold water. When the cauliflower is cool, drain again.

Peel the carrots and cut into ¼-inch sticks. Wash the celery and cut into pieces ¼ inch wide and 3 inches long. Trim the scallions. Rinse the tomatoes and pat dry.

Arrange the vegetables in a basket or on 4 serving plates and serve with a separate bowl of dip.

**SERVES 4**

## CREAMY ROQUEFORT DIP

### 26
CALORIES PER TABLESPOON

This pungent Roquefort concoction, which utilizes minimum calories to maximum effect, will delight even the most dedicated dieter! On the other hand, if you're feeling spendthrift with your calories, this creamy sauce might be used judiciously to dress up a simple endive salad.

    4  tablespoons plain low-fat yogurt
    6  tablespoons soft tofu
    6  tablespoons Roquefort or other blue cheese

Mash all ingredients together until smooth, or purée in a blender. Thin down, if necessary, with a little water. Serve chilled. This keeps well in the refrigerator for several days if stored in an airtight container.

**MAKES I CUP**

## WHOLE BOILED LOBSTERS WITH WILD RICE AND LEMON-BROCCOLI

### 411
CALORIES PER SERVING

This sumptuous dinner is lavish enough for the most important dinner company and would be suitable for a formal Spa dinner party—though perhaps it might be more appropriate for an *informal* dinner party. Whole-Wheat Berries with Scallions (page 107) would make a nice change from the wild rice.

This dish should be prepared restaurant-style; that is, cook the broccoli and wild rice well in advance and reheat just before serving, so that all your attention can be devoted to the lobsters. It's easiest to cook and reheat vegetables by placing them in a large strainer, which can quickly be plunged into boiling water.

    1½  cups wild rice, soaked overnight in cold water to cover, drained
        Vegetable seasoning to taste
    4  teaspoons sliced almonds
    1  small bunch broccoli

    4  quarts Fish Stock (page 161) or water
    4  (1½-pound) live lobsters

**GARNISH**
    2  lemons, quartered

TO PREPARE THE WILD RICE: Bring 1 quart of water to a boil, add the wild rice and vegetable seasoning, lower the heat, and cook at a rapid simmer for 15 to 20 minutes, or until the wild rice is tender but still slightly crunchy; begin to taste after 15 minutes. If the grains have started to pop open, the rice is overcooked. Drain and keep warm, or place in the top of the double boiler and reheat just before serving.

To brown the almonds, preheat the oven to 350°F. Scatter the almonds in a single layer on a small tray and bake for 3 to 5 minutes, or until golden brown. Set aside. (You may want to toast a larger quantity of almonds to keep on hand.)

TO PREPARE THE BROCCOLI: Cut off and discard the thick stems, leaving stalks about 4 to 5 inches long. You should have about 12 ounces of florets. Bring 2 quarts of water to a boil in a pot. Have ready a bowl of cold water. Add the florets to the boiling water and blanch for 2 minutes. Drain and immediately plunge into the bowl of cold water to stop the cooking and preserve the color. When the florets are cool, drain them, pat dry, and set aside.

TO PREPARE THE LOBSTERS: Put 2 quarts of fish stock in each of two large pots and bring to a boil. Put 2 lobsters in each pot, head first, cover, and return to a boil. Cook at a full boil for 10 minutes. When the lobsters have turned bright red, they are done.

When the lobsters are cooked, remove them from the broth with metal tongs or a long fork. Boiled lobsters leak a lot of juices; split them on a carving board with a grooved edge to catch the runoff, or on a large deep platter. (Lobsters cooked in water can simply be placed on 3 or 4 layers of paper towels, which will absorb the juices.) Turn each lobster on its back and, with a heavy knife, split it from head to tail. Open up the lobster, then remove and discard the sac between the eyes. Repeat for the 3 remaining lobsters. (If you have saved the juices, return them to the stock, strain, let cool, and freeze for future use.)

To serve, divide the wild rice equally among 4 large heated dinner plates and sprinkle a teaspoon of almonds over each portion. Place a lobster and a wedge of lemon on each plate. Reheat the broccoli florets in boiling water for 30 seconds, if necessary, drain, and serve on separate plates with another lemon wedge. Serve at once.

SERVES 4

# CRANBERRY-RASPBERRY MOUSSE

## 48
### CALORIES PER SERVING

We have chosen a light and slightly tart dessert to follow the rich lobster. This ethereal mousse looks and tastes so sophisticated, it's hard to believe how easy it is to prepare.

- ½ cup fresh or frozen cranberries
- ½ cup fresh or unsweetened frozen raspberries
- 1 pitted date, chopped
- ½ teaspoon water
- ¼ teaspoon arrowroot mixed with 1½ teaspoons fresh orange juice
- 1 tablespoon honey
- ⅛ teaspoon barley malt sweetener
- 1 recipe Spa Cream (page 27) made without sweetener

Put the cranberries, raspberries, date, and water in a saucepan and bring to a boil. Whisk in the arrowroot mixture, which acts as an instant thickener, and cook for 3 minutes. Force the fruit through a fine sieve to remove all the seeds. Add the honey and barley malt sweetener, let cool, and chill.

Just before serving, make Spa Cream. Fold the cream into the cold fruit purée, spoon into 4 chilled dessert bowls or glass goblets, and serve at once.

SERVES 4

# DAY 2

## BREAKFAST
### 158
#### CALORIES

HOT OATMEAL WITH
PRUNE AND APRICOT
COMPOTE AND YOGURT

HERBAL TEA OR
DECAFFEINATED COFFEE

## LUNCH
### 299
#### CALORIES

ITALIAN STUFFED
ZUCCHINI

CONCORD GRAPE MOUSSE

HERBAL TEA OR
DECAFFEINATED COFFEE

# HOT OATMEAL WITH PRUNE AND APRICOT COMPOTE AND YOGURT

## 158
### CALORIES PER SERVING

This old-fashioned country breakfast combines all the nutrients you need to get you through the morning. Prunes are an excellent source of iron, and apricots are rich in vitamin A. The fruits can easily be made the evening before, or even several days in advance. Keep them stored in the refrigerator in a tightly covered jar.

    4  prunes
    4  dried apricots
    ¾  cup water

    2  cups rolled oats
    1  quart water

    1  cup skim milk
    1⅓ cups plain low-fat yogurt

**TO PREPARE THE COMPOTE:** Put the prunes, apricots, and water in a small saucepan. Bring to a boil, lower the heat, and stew gently for 15 to 20 minutes.

**TO PREPARE OATMEAL:** Put the oatmeal and water in another saucepan, bring to a boil, reduce the heat to medium-low, and cook for 5 minutes, stirring constantly so that the oatmeal does not stick to the bottom of the pot.

Divide the oatmeal among 4 soup bowls and spoon an apricot and a prune with some of their juice over each portion. Pour ¼ cup of milk over each serving, and top with ⅓ cup of yogurt. Serve at once.

**SERVES 4**

# ITALIAN STUFFED ZUCCHINI

## 233
### CALORIES PER SERVING

Of Italian inspiration, this dish makes a dramatic presentation. Fresh zucchini are stuffed, quickly steamed, then sliced into decorative rounds, and arranged on a bright red background of garlicky tomato sauce and yogurt.

The dish photographed on the previous page was decorated by using a pastry bag to pipe thin lines of yogurt over the tomato sauce. The lines were then "feathered," a technique described below. If you have never played with a pastry bag before, do try it; it can be enjoyable. Practice first on wax paper until your hand is steady.

    4  medium zucchini
    1  tablespoon unsalted butter
    ¼  cup minced onion
    ½  garlic clove, minced
    8  mushrooms, coarsely chopped
    ¼  cup minced red bell pepper
    ½  pound spinach leaves, washed,
       patted dry, and coarsely chopped
    1  egg
    ½  cup whole-milk ricotta cheese
       Freshly ground white pepper to
       taste
       Vegetable seasoning to taste

    2  cups Garlicky Tomato Sauce
    ¼  cup plain low-fat yogurt

    4  teaspoons grated Asiago or
       Parmesan cheese
    ¼  cup peeled, seeded, and diced
       tomatoes

Cut the ends off the zucchini, then cut each piece in half crosswise, making 2 equal lengths. Using a melon baller or an apple corer, scoop out the seeds and pulp, leaving a shell about ¼ inch thick. Set aside the hollowed-out zucchini and reserve ¼ cup of the pulp.

Melt the butter in a skillet, add the onion and garlic, and sauté over medium-low heat for 3 minutes. Add the reserved zucchini pulp, mushrooms, red pepper, and chopped spinach, and sauté for 3 minutes more. Remove from the heat and let cool for several minutes. Add the egg, ricotta, white pepper, and vegetable seasoning, and mix well.

Pile the stuffing into a pastry bag fitted with a 1-inch plain nozzle. If you do not have a pastry bag, spoon the mixture into a heavyweight plastic freezer bag, forcing the stuffing down into one corner of the bag. With scissors, snip off enough of the corner to leave a 1-inch opening.

Take one of the zucchini and squeeze the stuffing into the open end until it is filled. Continue until all the zucchini pieces are stuffed.

Bring water to a boil in the bottom of a steamer. Place the zucchini in the top and steam for 4 to 6 minutes, or until cooked but still quite firm.

While the zucchini are cooking, spread ½ cup of tomato sauce in a circle over the bottom of each dinner plate. Put the yogurt in a pastry bag fitted with a fine plain tip, or spoon it into a small plastic bag, as with the zucchini mixture. Snip off a very small corner, so that only a fine line of yogurt will be forced through.

Squeeze the yogurt over the sauce in even horizontal lines, about I inch apart, until the plate is covered with stripes. Now "feather" the yogurt by drawing vertical lines through it with the point of a sharp knife. Start at one edge of the plate and move the knife from the top to the bottom of the plate, that is, toward you. As you do so, the yogurt will be pulled into little "Vs" pointing in the same direction as you pulled the knife. Draw another line, this time from bottom to top, about 1½ inches away from the first line. This time the "Vs" will point away from you. Continue drawing the knife through the sauce and yogurt, alternating the direction until the entire plate is covered with a beautiful red and white feathered design.

Remove the zucchini from the steamer and cut on the slant into slices ½ inch thick. Fan out the slices in a semicircle over half of each plate, sprinkle each portion with I teaspoon each grated cheese and diced tomatoes, and serve.

**SERVES 4**

# GARLICKY TOMATO SAUCE

## 66

### CALORIES PER ½ CUP

Our basic tomato sauce freezes well. Make double or triple quantities when tomatoes are in season and have a supply on hand throughout the year. It's wonderful on pasta, and it also adds spice to plain steamed vegetables. If the tomatoes in the market look truly luscious, omit the canned tomatoes and double the quantity of fresh.

- I tablespoon unsalted butter
- I onion, chopped
- 3 small garlic cloves, chopped (or to taste)
- 4 medium tomatoes, peeled, seeded, and coarsely chopped
- I cup imported canned plum tomatoes
- 3 medium carrots, peeled and cut into chunks
- ½ cup Chicken Stock (page 161) Freshly ground white pepper to taste Vegetable seasoning to taste

In a 2-quart saucepan, melt the butter, add the onion and garlic, and sauté for 3 minutes over medium-low heat. Add all the remaining ingredients, bring to a boil, lower the heat, and simmer, uncovered, for 30 minutes. Purée in a blender or food processor. Use 2 cups for Stuffed Zucchini, and freeze the rest for up to 8 months.

**MAKES I QUART**

# CONCORD GRAPE MOUSSE

## 66

### CALORIES PER SERVING

This deep violet mousse is sweet and satisfying—and astonishingly simple. Just remember to allow time for the juice mixture to cool—about an hour. Both the juice and the skim milk for the Spa Cream should be *very* cold for best results.

- I cup unsweetened Concord grape juice
- ⅛ teaspoon barley malt sweetener
- I tablespoon arrowroot mixed with 2 tablespoons grape juice
- I recipe Spa Cream (page 27) made without sweetener

In a small saucepan bring the grape juice and barley malt sweetener to a boil. Whisk in the arrowroot mixture, which will instantly thicken the juice, reduce the heat, and simmer, uncovered, for 2 minutes. Pour into a bowl, let cool, and chill in the refrigerator.

Make Spa Cream just before serving. Fold the cream into the cold grape mixture, spoon the mousse into 4 chilled dessert bowls or glass goblets, and serve at once.

**SERVES 4**

# DINNER
## 679
### CALORIES

LEEK AND POTATO SOUP
WITH CHIVES

INDIAN CHICKEN BROCHETTE WITH
LENTILS AND SNOW PEAS

CURRY SAUCE

NEW ORLEANS BAKED
BANANAS WITH ORANGE SAUCE

HERBAL TEA OR
DECAFFEINATED COFFEE

DAY 2

## LEEK AND POTATO SOUP WITH CHIVES

### 75
CALORIES PER SERVING

Leek and potato soup is reputed to be excellent for the complexion. This light soup is flavored with leeks, homemade chicken stock, onion, chives, and only a little potato—no cream at all! You can intensify the flavor by using Rich Chicken Stock (page 161). Consider making several quarts at once to have for emergencies; it freezes beautifully.

2  leeks, white part only
1  baking potato
1½  tablespoons unsalted butter
¼  cup chopped onion
1  quart Chicken Stock (page 161)
   Freshly ground white pepper to taste
   Vegetable seasoning to taste

### GARNISH
2  tablespoons chopped fresh chives

Wash the leeks carefully and chop coarsely. Peel the potato and cut into chunks. In a 2-quart pot, melt the butter and cook the leek over medium heat until softened. Add the potato, onion, and stock, and bring to a boil over high heat. Lower the heat and simmer, uncovered, for 30 minutes. Purée the soup in several batches in a blender or food processor. Season with pepper and vegetable seasoning and pour into 4 heated soup bowls. Sprinkle with the chopped chives and serve.

### SERVES 4

## INDIAN CHICKEN BROCHETTE WITH LENTILS AND SNOW PEAS

### 472
CALORIES PER SERVING

"Lavish" is the only way to describe this platter. The brochette, lentils, and snow peas should all be "prepped" (restaurant-kitchen terminology for advance preparation) hours before the meal is served. Accompany each portion with ½ cup of warm Curry Sauce.

1½  cups lentils
2  tablespoons minced fresh parsley
4  scallions, thinly sliced
   Freshly ground white pepper to taste
   Vegetable seasoning to taste
¾  pound snow peas
1  teaspoon unsalted butter
¼  teaspoon cold-pressed sesame oil
1½  pounds skinless, boneless chicken breasts
1  red, green, or yellow pepper, or a mixture
8  mushrooms
½  medium eggplant

**TO PREPARE THE LENTILS:** Put lentils in a pot with 1½ quarts of cold water, bring to a boil, lower the heat, and simmer, uncovered, for 30 to 40 minutes, or until they are tender but not mushy. Drain, put in a bowl, and mix with the chopped parsley and scallions. Season to taste. Keep warm, or reheat in the top of a double boiler just before serving.

**TO PREPARE THE SNOW PEAS:** While the lentils are cooking, remove the ends of the snow peas and string them. Have a bowl of cold water ready. Blanch the snow peas in 2 quarts of boiling water for 30 seconds. Drain and immediately plunge into the cold water to set the color and preserve the flavor. When the snow peas are cool, drain and pat dry. Just before the chicken is done, heat a sauté pan, add the butter, sesame oil, and snow peas, and toss for 1 minute to heat through.

**TO PREPARE THE BROCHETTES:** These can be prepared several hours before they are broiled. Remove any fat from the chicken breasts and cut them into 1-inch pieces. Cut the pepper into quarters, remove the stems, seeds, and whitish membranes, then cut each quarter in half crosswise. Cut off the mushroom stems (reserving the stems for stock). Without peeling, cut the eggplant into eight 1-inch cubes. Thread each of 4 bamboo or metal skewers with one quarter of the chicken and 2 pieces each pepper, mushrooms, and eggplant. If prepared ahead, place the skewers on a plate, cover tightly with plastic wrap, and refrigerate.

Preheat the broiler.

Broil the chicken brochettes for 4 to 6 minutes on each side. Chicken cooks quickly when it is cut into small pieces, so be careful not to let it burn or dry it out.

To serve, divide the lentils among 4 heated dinner plates, then place a brochette and a portion of snow peas on each plate. Serve with separate bowls of Curry Sauce.

### SERVES 4

# CURRY SAUCE

## 56
CALORIES PER ½ CUP

This rich spicy sauce, thickened with a purée of fruits and vegetables, is an excellent accompaniment to roasted or broiled chicken, steamed vegetables, and brown rice or wild rice. Like saffron, curry powder must be cooked in a little butter or oil to release its flavor.

2 tablespoons unsalted butter
1 onion, coarsely chopped
½ celery stalk, coarsely chopped
1 carrot, peeled and coarsely chopped
1 garlic clove, minced
1 red Delicious apple, peeled, cored, and coarsely chopped
½ banana, peeled and sliced
2 tablespoons curry powder
1½ teaspoons tomato purée
1 sprig Italian parsley
1½ teaspoons unsweetened shredded coconut (optional)
2 cups Rich Chicken Stock (page 161)
Dash of cayenne pepper or drops of Tabasco sauce to taste
¼ cup whole milk
1 to 3 additional tablespoons curry powder (optional)
1 teaspoon unsalted butter (optional)

Melt the butter in a 2-quart saucepan, add the onion, celery, carrot, garlic, apple, and banana, and sauté over medium heat for 5 minutes. Add the curry powder and tomato purée and cook for 3 minutes more, stirring often. Add the parsley, coconut, and stock and bring to a boil. Lower the heat and simmer the sauce, uncovered, for 1 hour, stirring often so that the vegetables and fruit do not stick to the bottom of the pan.

Strain the sauce into a small bowl, reserving liquids and solids separately. Purée the fruit and vegetables in a blender or food processor with a little of the liquid, then return the purée and liquid to the saucepan. Add the cayenne pepper and milk, and warm over low heat. *Do not boil.* Taste the sauce for seasoning. Curry becomes milder the longer you cook it. If you prefer a stronger curry flavor, sauté 1 to 3 tablespoons of curry powder in 1 teaspoon of butter for about 3 minutes, stirring constantly so that the mixture does not burn. Add ½ cup of sauce to the pan and stir to incorporate all the curry into the liquid, then return to the larger pot.

Pour 2 cups of sauce into a serving bowl for the chicken brochettes; cool and freeze the remainder for up to 6 months. Freezing will diminish the curry flavor, so taste the sauce when you reheat it.

**MAKES ABOUT 3½ CUPS**

# NEW ORLEANS BAKED BANANAS WITH ORANGE SAUCE

## 76
CALORIES PER SERVING

In the West Indies, this potassium-rich fruit (or, often, plantain) is prepared many different ways. Our version is baked in foil with honey and butter, scented with orange and vanilla. The aroma from the just-opened package is heavenly!

2 bananas
1 tablespoon grated orange rind
1 tablespoon honey
1 tablespoon fresh orange juice
1 teaspoon vanilla extract
1 teaspoon unsalted butter, cut into 4 pieces

### GARNISH
Julienned orange rind (optional)
1 vanilla bean, cut into 4 pieces (optional)

Preheat the oven to 350°F. Cut 4 pieces of foil, each 4 x 6 inches.

Peel the bananas, cut them in half lengthwise, and place each half on a foil rectangle. In a small bowl, mix the orange rind, honey, orange juice, and vanilla extract, and spoon over the banana halves. Top each half with a piece of butter. Fold over the foil once and crimp the ends to seal. Place on a baking sheet and bake for 5 to 8 minutes; if the bananas are really ripe, they will cook in about 5 minutes.

To serve, slash the bananas in 5 places along the outside edge and curve into semicircles. Pour the juices over the fruit and garnish with orange rind and vanilla bean.

**SERVES 4**

# DAY 3

## BREAKFAST
### 411
#### CALORIES

SONOMA FRITTATA

HONEYED PEAR BUTTER

GRANDMA'S
WHOLE-WHEAT BREAD

HERBAL TEA OR
DECAFFEINATED COFFEE

## LUNCH
### 271
#### CALORIES

CALIFORNIA MINESTRONE

HOT ITALIAN PLUM
COMPOTE

HERBAL TEA OR
DECAFFEINATED COFFEE

## SONOMA FRITTATA

### 180

CALORIES PER SERVING

Frittata, an open-faced Italian omelet, can accommodate a wide range of fillings. Sautéed zucchini, fennel, and blanched asparagus or broccoli are only a few of many possible additions. Combined with our Vichyssoise and a tossed green salad, this would make an admirable light summer meal.

- 1 teaspoon unsalted butter
- ½ cup chopped onion
- ½ green pepper, cut into ¼-inch dice
- 1 unpeeled tomato, seeded and chopped
- 8 eggs
  Freshly ground white pepper to taste
  Vegetable seasoning to taste

Preheat the oven to 400°F.

In a 6- to 8-inch nonstick skillet, melt the butter, add the onion and green pepper, and sauté over low heat, stirring often, for about 4 minutes, or until half cooked. Add the tomato and cook for 2 minutes more, then remove from the heat.

Crack the eggs into a bowl and whisk for 1 minute. Add the sautéed vegetables and mix, then pour into a nonstick ovenproof pan and bake for 4 to 6 minutes, or until the mixture rises and is firm in the center. When the eggs are done, season them with pepper and vegetable seasoning.

While the frittata is baking, toast the bread. Cut the frittata into quarters and serve on heated plates with 2 slices of toast and a small bowl of Honeyed Pear Butter.

SERVES 4

## HONEYED PEAR BUTTER

### 75

CALORIES PER SERVING

Soft ripe pears make a smoother, sweeter spread. Like our other breakfast spreads, Honeyed Pear Butter, tightly covered, keeps well in the refrigerator for up to 2 weeks, so you might want to double or triple this recipe. Each tablespoon has 25 calories.

- 2 pears, peeled, cored, and chopped
- ½ cup water
- ⅛ teaspoon ground cinnamon
- 1 teaspoon unsalted butter
- 1 tablespoon honey

Put all ingredients in a small saucepan and cook over medium-low heat for 15 to 20 minutes, or until pears are tender, stirring often. Purée the fruit and spread 1½ tablespoons on each slice of bread, two per person.

SERVES 4

## GRANDMA'S WHOLE-WHEAT BREAD

### 78

CALORIES PER ½-INCH SLICE

At the Spa we use 100 percent stone-ground whole-wheat flour for all our breads, muffins, and pasta. Stone grinding, a much slower process than the usual steel-roller method, protects the germ of the wheat and preserves more of its nutritional value. You can knead this simplified version of our Sonoma Valley bread by hand or use an electric mixer with a dough hook. This Spa bread can be made ahead and frozen, without losing its nutritional benefits.

- 2½ cups warm water (about 110°F.)
- 2 tablespoons date sugar
- 1 tablespoon dry yeast
- 6 cups stone-ground whole-wheat flour
- 1 teaspoon vegetable seasoning

Pour the warm water into the large bowl of an electric mixer, stir in the date sugar, and sprinkle the yeast over the top. After 5 to 10 minutes, when the yeast has begun to bubble, stir in 3 cups of the flour and, with the dough hook, mix at low speed until smooth. Add the vegetable seasoning and the remaining flour, a cup at a time, and continue to knead until the dough pulls away from the sides of the bowl and is smooth and elastic, about 10 minutes. Turn the dough out on a very lightly floured work surface and knead by hand two or three times. Scrape out the mixer bowl and butter it very lightly. Form the dough into a ball and turn it in the bowl so that it is greased on all sides. Cover the bowl with a towel, and place the bowl in a warm spot (an oven with the pilot light on, for instance). Leave until the dough has doubled in bulk, about 60 to 75 minutes.

Punch down the dough and cut in half. Form into loaves and place in two nonstick or lightly greased 8-inch loaf pans. Cover with a towel and leave in a warm place to rise until doubled in bulk, about 45 minutes.

Preheat the oven to 375°F. Bake the loaves for 40 minutes, and turn out onto racks to cool. Cut each loaf into 16 slices and freeze, 2 or 4 slices to a foil package. We serve single-slice portions for the breakfast on the 850-calorie menu and 1 or 2 slices for the 1,200-calorie menu.

MAKES TWO 8-INCH LOAVES

## CALIFORNIA MINESTRONE

### 150
CALORIES PER SERVING

In our version of minestrone, the great Italian soup, a medley of fresh vegetables is simmered in homemade broth. As a final touch, the soup is enhanced by a teaspoon of pesto added just before serving.

- 1 tablespoon unsalted butter
- ½ onion, cut into ½-inch dice
- 1 leek (white part only), washed and cut into ¼-inch slices
- 1 carrot, peeled and cut into ¼-inch slices
- 1 celery stalk, cut into ¼-inch slices
- 1 garlic clove, minced
- 2 unpeeled tomatoes, seeded and chopped, or 3 to 4 canned plum tomatoes, drained
- 4 cabbage leaves, coarsely chopped
- 6 ounces fresh green beans, ends trimmed and cut on the slant into ½-inch pieces
- 2 quarts Chicken Stock (page 161)
- 10 spinach leaves, washed, drained, and coarsely chopped
  Freshly ground white pepper to taste
  Vegetable seasoning to taste
- 1 teaspoon Spa Pesto
- ¼ cup grated Asiago or Parmesan cheese

In a 4-quart pot, melt the butter, add the onion, leek, carrot, celery, garlic, tomatoes, cabbage, and green beans, and sauté over medium heat for 3 to 5 minutes, stirring often. Add the stock and bring to a boil. Lower the heat and simmer, uncovered, for 25 minutes. Add the spinach and simmer for 5 more minutes. Taste the finished soup and adjust the seasonings. Remove the pot from the burner and stir in the pesto. Serve in large heated soup bowls and sprinkle 1 tablespoon of grated cheese over each portion.

**SERVES 4**

## SPA PESTO

### 11
CALORIES PER TABLESPOON

Fragrant Spa Pesto is heady with garlic and fresh basil, but made without nuts or cheese and with only 1 tablespoon of olive oil. Make several batches during the summer, when fresh young basil is plentiful. Frozen in ice cube trays, the pesto can be used year-round in soups, sauces, and in our hot pasta salad (page 47).

- 2 cups fresh basil leaves, washed and patted dry
- 6 very large garlic cloves, minced
- 1 tablespoon extra-virgin olive oil

Purée all the ingredients in a blender or food processor. Keep frozen pesto cubes in a freezer bag to avoid freezer burn. Defrosted, each cube will yield about 2 tablespoons.

**MAKES ABOUT 1 CUP**

## HOT ITALIAN PLUM COMPOTE

### 121
CALORIES PER SERVING

This dessert tastes especially good made with Italian plums, which are easily pitted and hold their shape well.

- 8 large Italian purple plums
- ⅛ teaspoon ground cinnamon
- 1 tablespoon honey
- ½ cup fresh orange juice
- ⅛ teaspoon vanilla extract
  Barley malt sweetener to taste

Wash the plums, cut in half, and remove the pits. Put them in a saucepan with all the remaining ingredients except the barley malt sweetener. Bring to a boil, remove from the heat, and taste for sweetness. Add barley malt sweetener, if necessary. Serve at once.

**SERVES 4**

# DAY 3

### D I N N E R
### 456
#### CALORIES

ROMAINE AND SNOW PEA SALAD

RASPBERRY VINAIGRETTE

POACHED BASS PROVENÇAL
WITH GARDEN VEGETABLES

ANJOU PEARS WITH
ORANGE ZABAGLIONE

HERBAL TEA OR DECAFFEINATED COFFEE

## ROMAINE AND SNOW PEA SALAD

### 93

CALORIES PER SERVING

This crisp refreshing salad is dressed up with a raspberry vinaigrette to make an elegant first course. The faint perfume of raspberries adds another dimension to the classic vinaigrette.

1 large head romaine lettuce
32 snow peas, ends trimmed and strings removed
½ cup Raspberry Vinaigrette

Wash the romaine, discarding wilted and damaged leaves, but do not separate the remaining leaves from the head. Pat dry before cutting the head into quarters.

Have a bowl of cold water ready. Blanch the snow peas in a quart of boiling water for 30 seconds, then drain and immediately plunge them into the cold water. When they are cool, drain again and pat dry.

Arrange the romaine quarters and snow peas on 4 large salad plates and sprinkle each portion with 2 tablespoons of Raspberry Vinaigrette.

**SERVES 4**

## RASPBERRY VINAIGRETTE

### 35

CALORIES PER TABLESPOON

Fragrant and slightly sweet, raspberry vinegar can be bought at most gourmet food shops and 2 tablespoons of this aromatic blend will make any salad special. This dressing can be stored, tightly covered, in the refrigerator for up to a week.

¼ cup cold-pressed safflower oil
5 tablespoons red raspberry vinegar
¼ cup water
2 tablespoons fresh or thawed frozen raspberries
1 tablespoon lime juice
1 tablespoon minced shallots
1½ teaspoons sesame oil
⅛ teaspoon vegetable seasoning Dash of Tabasco sauce

Mix all the ingredients and refrigerate in a tightly covered jar for at least 1 hour before using.

**MAKES ABOUT 1 CUP**

## POACHED BASS PROVENÇAL WITH GARDEN VEGETABLES

### 251

CALORIES PER SERVING

A hearty combination of meaty striped bass fillets, fresh al dente vegetables, and a Provençal fish broth. Any flavorful, firm-fleshed fish fillets may be substituted, such as halibut, salmon, red snapper, or tilefish. Sole or flounder would make a milder dish.

1½ pounds sea bass or striped bass fillets (2 fillets)
1 recipe Saffron-Tomato Fish Broth
2½ tablespoons unsalted butter
1 medium carrot, peeled
1 medium turnip, peeled
1 large celery stalk
1 medium leek (white part only), well washed

Preheat the oven to 350°F.

Cut each bass fillet in half and lay the fish in a single layer in a shallow baking pan. Reserve 2 tablespoons of the broth and pour the rest over the fillets. Cover the pan with foil and crimp tightly around the edges to seal. Bake for 8 to 10 minutes, or until the fish flakes easily.

While the fish is poaching, cut all the vegetables into strips 2 inches long by ¼ inch wide. Melt the butter in a nonstick sauté pan and add all the vegetables and the reserved broth. Sauté for 2 to 3 minutes over medium heat, stirring constantly.

To serve, divide the vegetables among 4 heated wide soup bowls. With a spatula, lift the fish fillets from the broth and place over each nest of vegetables. Gently pour the broth over the fish and serve.

**SERVES 4**

# SAFFRON-TOMATO FISH BROTH

## 34
### CALORIES PER CUP

An aromatic broth based on Proven-çal seasonings—olive oil, garlic, saffron, and tomatoes. Served plain, it would make an elegant soup course for a special dinner. At our Monte Carlo spa we use it as a delicious steaming liquid for clams and mussels.

 1 tablespoon extra-virgin olive oil
 1 carrot, peeled and coarsely chopped
 1 celery stalk, coarsely chopped
 ¼ cup chopped onion
 ¾ cup chopped mushrooms
 ¼ cup chopped white of leek
 3 garlic cloves, minced
 8 ounces scallops (optional)
 ¼ cup dry white wine
 2 pinches Spanish saffron threads
 2 tomatoes, chopped, or 3 or 4 canned plum tomatoes, drained
 1 sprig Italian parsley
 6 cups Fish Stock (page 160)

Heat the olive oil in a large stockpot, add the carrot, celery, onion, mushrooms, leek, and garlic, and sauté over medium heat for 4 minutes, stirring often. Add the scallops, wine, saffron, tomatoes, and parsley, and sauté for 2 minutes more, stirring. Add the stock, bring to a boil, and reduce over medium-high heat for 5 minutes only. (Longer cooking diminishes the pungent flavors of garlic and saffron.) Strain the broth, discarding the solids, and let cool, uncovered, to room temperature.

**MAKES ABOUT 5 CUPS**

# ANJOU PEARS WITH ORANGE ZABAGLIONE

## 112
### CALORIES PER SERVING

Gently poached Anjou pears are flavored with cinnamon, honey, and vanilla and served with an extravagant Orange Zabaglione spiked with Grand Marnier. This elegant dessert is the perfect climax for a sumptuous Spa dinner party. If you're planning ahead, the poaching liquid can be made several days in advance and the pears can be cooked the day before, but the zabaglione must be whisked at the last minute, just before serving, to maintain its frothy finesse.

## POACHING LIQUID
 1 quart water
 1 tablespoon vanilla extract
 2 tablespoons honey
 ¼ teaspoon barley malt sweetener (optional)
 ¼ cup white wine
 1 cinnamon stick
 ⅛ teaspoon ground coriander

 2 slightly underripe Anjou pears

## ORANGE ZABAGLIONE
 2 egg yolks
 ¼ teaspoon vanilla extract
 1½ teaspoons Grand Marnier
 2 teaspoons grated orange rind
 ¼ cup fresh orange juice
 1½ teaspoons honey
   Pinch of barley malt sweetener (optional)

## GARNISH
   Finely julienned orange rind
 4 lemon leaf sprigs

Combine all poaching liquid ingredients in a saucepan. Bring to a boil, then reduce heat and simmer for 10 minutes. Strain the mixture and let cool.

Cut the pears in half lengthwise and core. Place in a wide saucepan, cut side down, and cover with the cooled poaching liquid. Bring to a boil, lower the heat, and simmer, uncovered, until the pears are tender but still somewhat firm, about 3 to 5 minutes, depending on the ripeness of your pears. Remove from the heat and let stand while you prepare the zabaglione.

In the top of a double boiler or in a metal mixing bowl (copper is best), combine all the zabaglione ingredients. Whisk constantly over simmering water until the sauce is thickened and foamy, about 5 minutes. Remove the bowl from the water to keep the eggs from coagulating.

Spoon 2 tablespoons of zabaglione on each of 4 serving plates and arrange the pears over the sauce, cut side down. Decorate with the orange rind and lemon sprigs and serve at once.

**SERVES 4**

# DAY 4

## BREAKFAST
### 154
#### CALORIES

BREAKFAST CRÊPES WITH
FRESH STRAWBERRY
PURÉE AND
ORANGE-YOGURT SAUCE

HERBAL TEA OR
DECAFFEINATED COFFEE

*for company
@breakfast*

## LUNCH
### 536
#### CALORIES

BULGUR WITH GINGER
AND SCALLIONS

WALNUT PÂTÉ

NEW ENGLAND HOT
SPICED APPLE CIDER

# BREAKFAST CRÊPES WITH FRESH STRAWBERRY PURÉE AND ORANGE-YOGURT SAUCE

## 154
### CALORIES PER SERVING

Inspired by the classic French dessert crêpe, this nutrition-packed treat is filled with cottage cheese and fresh sliced strawberries, and served with two sauces. This breakfast gets rave reviews from our Spa guests and makes a perfect Sunday brunch dish for company, since almost everything can be made ahead and assembled at the last minute. The versatile yogurt sauce has a mere 16 calories per tablespoon.

### ORANGE-YOGURT SAUCE

    ½  cup plain low-fat yogurt
    1  tablespoon fresh orange juice
    ½  teaspoon grated orange rind
    ½  teaspoon grated lemon rind
    2  teaspoons honey
    ⅛  teaspoon freshly grated nutmeg
       Pinch of ground mace
       Pinch of barley malt sweetener
       (optional)

    8  Spa Crêpes
    1  cup low-fat cottage cheese
    ¾  cup sliced fresh strawberries, or a
       mixture of strawberries, orange
       segments, and sliced rind
    ½  cup strained puréed strawberries
       (about ¾ cup whole strawberries)
    1  kiwi fruit, peeled and cut into 8
       slices
    2  fresh strawberries, sliced

To make the yogurt sauce, whisk all the ingredients in a small mixing bowl, cover, and store in the refrigerator. If the sauce seems too thick to pour, thin it with water, added a spoonful at a time.

If the crêpes were made in advance, preheat the oven to 350°F. Spread the crêpes in a single layer on a baking sheet and bake for 3 to 5 minutes, until warm but not dried out.

For each portion, fold 2 crêpes in half and place on a serving plate with straight sides touching. Lift up the tops of the crêpes and spread 2 tablespoons of cottage cheese over the bottom half of each. Place 1½ tablespoons of sliced strawberries over the cottage cheese on each crêpe and fold down the tops of the crêpes. Spread 2 tablespoons of yogurt sauce around the edge of one of the crêpes and 2 tablespoons of strawberry purée around the other. Place 2 kiwi slices and 2 strawberry slices in the center of the crêpes and serve.

**SERVES 4**

# SPA CRÊPES

## 25
### CALORIES PER CRÊPE

We often serve these delicate crêpes for breakfast, but they would also make an elegant dessert, served with sliced fresh fruit and topped with Spa Cream (page 27). The secret to great crêpes is letting the batter sit overnight. You can even start making the crêpes 2 days before you serve them, preparing the batter the first day and cooking the crêpes the following day. Wrapped in plastic wrap or wax paper, they will keep for 2 or 3 days in the refrigerator. They can also be made in large batches and frozen for up to a month; they defrost in only a few minutes. For this recipe you will need whole-wheat pastry flour and al-

mond oil, both available in health food stores.

    1    whole egg
    2    egg whites
    1¼   cup nonfat skim milk
    ¾    cup stone-ground whole-wheat
         pastry flour
    ¼    cup unbleached white flour
    2    teaspoons toasted wheat germ
    1½   tablespoons almond oil
    1    teaspoon ground cinnamon
    ½    teaspoon vanilla extract
         Pinch of barley malt sweetener

In a blender, combine all the ingredients and blend for 1 minute. Pour into another container, cover, and let the batter stand, unrefrigerated, for at least 8 hours, or preferably overnight in the refrigerator.

Check the consistency of the batter before you cook the crêpes; it should be no thicker than heavy cream. If necessary, stir in more skim milk, a spoonful at a time, until you have the right consistency.

Place a 5- to 6-inch nonstick crêpe pan over moderately high heat and, using a pastry brush, very lightly grease the pan with cold-pressed vegetable oil. Pour in 2 to 3 tablespoons of batter and quickly tilt the pan in all directions until the batter is evenly distributed over the surface. Cook until the underside is golden, about 30 seconds, turn, and cook the other side for 10 seconds. Continue to cook the crêpes, greasing the pan only when necessary. Stack the crêpes in batches of 8. Use immediately, or, when they are cool, wrap in plastic wrap and refrigerate for up to 3 days or freeze for up to 1 month. (Crêpes should be defrosted in the refrigerator, then reheated for 10 minutes, wrapped in foil in a warm oven.)

**MAKES 32**

# BULGUR WITH GINGER AND SCALLIONS

## 256

CALORIES PER SERVING

Marinated tofu lends a good touch to the bulgur. To serve with the Walnut Pâté, marinate the tofu and cook the bulgur in advance. The bulgur may be kept warm in the top of a double boiler. Arrange the roasted peppers attractively on the pâté slice and surround them with bulgur.

- 2 tablespoons low-sodium soy sauce
  Pinch of ground ginger
- 1 teaspoon honey
- 1 square firm tofu, cut into ¼-inch dice
- 1½ cups bulgur
- 1 tablespoon unsalted butter
- 4 scallions (white and green parts), thinly sliced
- 2 tablespoons chopped Italian parsley
- 2 red peppers, roasted and peeled, or 1 jar of pimientos
- 1 avocado, pitted, peeled, and sliced
- 8 radishes, stem and root ends trimmed

In a small bowl, mix the soy sauce, ginger, and honey. Add the tofu and marinate for 1 hour.

Cook the bulgur, uncovered, in 4 to 6 cups of rapidly simmering water for 30 minutes. Strain and keep warm.

Melt the butter over low heat in a 6- to 8-inch sauté pan, add the scallions, and toss for 2 minutes. Add the bulgur and stir for 2 minutes more. Drain the tofu and add it to the bulgur with the parsley; stir gently for 1 minute. Add to each portion some avocado, radishes, and roast peppers and serve.

SERVES 4

# WALNUT PÂTE

## 163

CALORIES PER ½-INCH SLICE

This flavorful, nutty pâté forms the centerpiece of our rich luncheon salad, with good reason—it's absolutely delicious! We serve it at room temperature for lunch or as a hot stuffing for green peppers. It would also make a good party hors d'oeuvre. The pâté may be stored in the refrigerator for 2 or 3 days, well covered with plastic wrap.

- ½ pound spinach
- ¼ cup olive oil
- 2 small yellow onions, cut into ¼-inch dice
- 1 garlic clove, minced
- 2 cups ground walnuts
- 1 cup dry whole-wheat bread crumbs
- ½ cup raw wheat germ
- 3 eggs, beaten
- ¼ cup chopped Italian parsley
- 1 teaspoon dried oregano
- ¼ teaspoon dried thyme
- ½ teaspoon ground cumin
- 1 medium unpeeled tomato, seeded and chopped
- 1 tablespoon low-sodium soy sauce

Preheat the oven to 350°F. Lightly oil a 9 × 5 × 3-inch loaf pan, or use a nonstick pan.

Remove the stems from the spinach. Wash the leaves well, pat dry, and chop coarsely.

Heat the olive oil in a skillet, add the onions and garlic, and sauté over medium-high heat, stirring constantly, until the vegetables just start to brown. Add the spinach, toss for 1 minute, and transfer to a mixing bowl.

Add all the remaining ingredients and mix gently until just combined. Pack into the baking pan and bake for 35 to 45 minutes. Set on a rack and let the pâté cool to room temperature in the pan, about 1 hour.

MAKES ONE 9-INCH LOAF

# NEW ENGLAND HOT SPICED APPLE CIDER

## 117

CALORIES PER SERVING

The aroma of cinnamon and cloves with hot mulled apple cider is as much a part of the New England fall as turning leaves. Coriander seeds add extra zing to this spicy drink. At the Spa we use crisp ripe apples put through the juicer, but unsweetened bottled apple juice is a fine substitute. Fresh apple juice can be bought at any health-food store with a juice bar.

- 1 quart fresh or bottled apple juice (6 to 8 apples put through the juicer)
- 1 cinnamon stick
- 2 whole cloves
- 4 whole coriander seeds

Put all the ingredients in a saucepan and bring to a boil. Reduce the heat and simmer, uncovered, for 4 to 5 minutes. Serve in mugs.

SERVES 4

# DAY 4

# DINNER
## 507
### CALORIES

CURRIED CARROT SOUP
WITH CHIVES

SEAFOOD SAUSAGES

HERB BUTTER FONDUE

SAUTÉED SWISS CHARD

SPA GÉNOISES

HERBAL TEA OR
DECAFFEINATED COFFEE

# CURRIED CARROT SOUP WITH CHIVES

## 66
### CALORIES PER SERVING

A bright soup to add color and flavor to any dinner or lunch, our curried carrot soup can be prepared well in advance and reheated just before serving.

  1  tablespoon unsalted butter
  ½  onion, coarsely chopped
  4  carrots, peeled and coarsely chopped
  1  celery stalk, coarsely chopped
  ½  garlic clove, minced
  3  tablespoons curry powder
  6  cups Chicken Stock (page 161)
     Freshly ground white pepper to taste
     Vegetable seasoning to taste

### GARNISH
  2  tablespoons chopped chives

In a 3-quart pot, melt the butter, add the chopped vegetables and garlic, and sauté for 4 minutes over medium heat, stirring often. Add the curry powder and cook for 3 minutes more, stirring constantly. Do not allow the curry to burn. Add the stock, turn up the heat to high, and bring to a boil. Lower the heat and simmer, uncovered, for 30 minutes. Purée the soup in several batches in a blender or food processor and return to the pot. Season to taste. The soup can be made ahead to this point.

To serve, reheat the soup, pour into 4 warmed soup bowls, and sprinkle with chives.

### SERVES 4

# SEAFOOD SAUSAGES

## 204
### CALORIES PER SERVING

One of our most popular creations, this special sausage is a staple at all our Spas. Delicate sole mousse is mixed with fresh herbs, diced seafood, and sautéed greens, then gently poached in fish stock. We usually serve the sausages hot with Herb Butter Fondue, but they are also good cold accompanied by Saffron Mayonnaise (page 55) or sliced into rounds for hors d'oeuvres.

 12  ounces spinach
  ½  bunch watercress
  1  teaspoon unsalted butter
  2  tablespoons minced shallots
  6  ounces fillet of sole
  1  egg white
  2  tablespoons nonfat skim milk
  8  ounces mixed boneless fish or shellfish (shrimps, scallops, lobster, salmon, halibut), cut into ¼-inch dice
  1  teaspoon chopped fresh tarragon or dill
  1  teaspoon chopped fresh chives
     Freshly ground white pepper to taste
     Pinch of freshly grated nutmeg
     Vegetable seasoning to taste
  4  small new red potatoes, scrubbed
  2  quarts Fish Stock (page 160) or water

### GARNISH
  1  cucumber, peeled, seeded, and cut into thin julienne strips
  1  tablespoon chopped fresh parsley

Cut off and discard the spinach and watercress stems, wash the leaves, pat them dry, and chop coarsely. In a nonstick skillet, melt the butter, add the shallots, and sauté over medium-low heat for 2 minutes. Add the spinach and watercress and toss for 1 minute. Transfer to a mixing bowl and refrigerate until very cold.

To make the mousse, purée the sole in a food processor for 30 seconds, add the egg white, and process for 15 seconds. Stop the machine and scrape down the bowl, then process for 15 seconds more, adding the milk gradually while the machine is running. Put the mousse in a bowl, cover with plastic wrap, and refrigerate.

When the spinach and watercress are cold, mix them with the mousse, diced fish, chopped herbs, pepper, nutmeg, and vegetable seasoning.

Cut 4 foil rectangles, 8 × 6 inches. Lightly butter or oil one side of the foil and place one quarter of the fish and vegetables close to a long edge of each piece. Form into cylinders about 4 inches long and 1½ inches thick. Roll up the sausages in the foil and twist the ends to seal. As you twist, the filling will be pushed toward the center. The sausages can be prepared ahead to this point and refrigerated.

Begin cooking the potatoes before you poach the sausages. Wash the potatoes and put them in a pot with cold water to cover. Bring to a boil over high heat, lower the flame, and cook at a rapid simmer for about 15 minutes, or until fork-tender.

Bring the stock to a fast simmer, add the foil packets, and simmer for 6 to 8 minutes. Do not allow the stock to boil. Remove the sausages from the stock with a slotted spoon and unwrap them. (Cool and freeze the stock for future use.)

To serve, slice the potatoes and arrange on 4 heated plates. Arrange sausages and cucumber on the plates. Pour 1 tablespoon of Herb Butter Fondue over each sausage, sprinkle with parsley, and serve.

### SERVES 4

# HERB BUTTER FONDUE

## 107
### CALORIES PER TABLESPOON

A savory sauce with a creamy consistency, our herb butter can be used sparingly but frequently with poached fish of any kind.

- 1 tablespoon minced shallots
- 1 ½ tablespoons white wine or dry vermouth
- 2 ½ teaspoons mild white wine vinegar
- 4 tablespoons (½ stick) unsalted butter, at room temperature
- ½ tablespoon mixed chopped fresh herbs (tarragon, chives, basil, parsley, dill)

Put the shallots, wine, and vinegar in a small saucepan, set over high heat, and reduce to ½ teaspoon of liquid. Remove from the heat and cool for 1 or 2 minutes. The reduction should still be quite warm but not hot.

Return the pan to a very low heat and begin whisking in the butter, a tablespoon at a time, moving the pan off the burner if the sauce becomes too hot. The butter will become creamy, but should not melt. When all the butter has been incorporated, whisk in the herbs.

This sauce can be prepared hours ahead of time and kept warm over a bowl of warm, not hot, water. Replace the warm water from time to time as it cools off. Whisk the sauce again before serving.

**MAKES ABOUT ¼ CUP**

# SAUTÉED SWISS CHARD

## 40
### CALORIES PER SERVING

Similar to spinach in flavor and texture, Swiss chard need be cooked only briefly. If chard is not in season, use 1 ½ pounds tender young spinach instead.

- 1 bunch Swiss chard
- 1 tablespoon olive oil
  Freshly ground white pepper to taste
  Vegetable seasoning to taste

Cut the heavy white stems from the Swiss chard, all the way up to the leaves, and discard the stems. Wash the leaves in a sink filled with cold water, swirling the chard to loosen the sand. Lift out of the water into a colander, leaving the sand at the bottom of the sink. Rinse the leaves again under cold running water.

In a pot, bring 1 quart of water to a boil, add the chard, and blanch for 10 seconds. Drain in a colander and refresh under cold running water. With your hands, squeeze out as much water as possible.

Pour the oil into a 6- to 8-inch sauté pan, preferably nonstick. Over medium heat, add the chard and toss for 2 minutes. Season with pepper and vegetable seasoning and serve.

**SERVES 4**

# SPA GÉNOISES

## 90
### CALORIES PER GÉNOISE

These light little cakes are the Spa's answer to génoise, the buttery French spongecake. Because whole-wheat flour is heavier than refined white flour, we use baking powder without aluminum in addition to the eggs as leavening. Eaten by themselves, the cakes are an earthly pleasure; embellished with ripe berries or peaches and Spa Cream, they are heavenly.

- 4 eggs, at room temperature
- ⅓ cup brown sugar
- 1 tablespoon grated lemon rind
- 1 teaspoon vanilla extract
- ⅔ cup stone-ground whole-wheat flour
- 1 teaspoon baking powder
- ⅛ teaspoon barley malt sweetener
- 1 ½ tablespoons unsalted butter, melted and cooled

## GARNISH
- 4 strips of lemon peel
- 4 lemon leaf sprigs

Preheat the oven to 350°F. Lightly butter twelve 1-cup muffin forms, dust them with whole-wheat flour, and shake out excess flour.

Break the eggs into the bowl of an electric mixer, add the sugar, lemon rind and vanilla, and whip at high speed until the eggs have doubled in volume and are lemon-colored, about 5 minutes.

Sift the flour, baking powder, and barley malt sweetener into another bowl.

When the eggs have doubled in volume, remove the bowl from the mixer stand. Sprinkle the flour mixture and the butter over the eggs and fold in, using a rubber spatula. Fill the muffin tins and bake for 20 minutes. Put the forms on cake racks and allow the génoises to cool. Serve four génoises, decorated with lemon peel and sprigs. Wrap the remaining 8 individually in foil, and freeze for up to a month, to be defrosted at room temperature and served immediately.

**MAKES 12**

# DAY 5

## BREAKFAST
### 173
#### CALORIES

MELON BALLS AND
STRAWBERRIES WITH
FRESH MINT

SONOMA BRAN MUFFINS

HERBAL TEA OR
DECAFFEINATED COFFEE

## LUNCH
### 233
#### CALORIES

ARTICHOKES WITH
CHICKPEA SALAD AND
LEMON MAYONNAISE

WARM HONEY-GLAZED
PINEAPPLE

HERBAL TEA OR
DECAFFEINATED COFFEE

# MELON BALLS AND STRAWBERRIES WITH FRESH MINT

## 58
### CALORIES PER SERVING

A bright way to start the day, this high-energy fruit cup is loaded with vitamins A and C and potassium.

24  medium strawberries
1  cantaloupe

## GARNISH

4  mint sprigs

Wash the strawberries only if they are sandy. Hull them and slice into thirds lengthwise. Put the slices in a bowl.

Cut the cantaloupe in half and scrape out the seeds. Scoop into the flesh with a round melon-baller, keeping the indentations close together to get as many balls as possible. Add the melon to the strawberries. With a spoon, scrape out any pulp and juice remaining in the cantaloupe shells and place in the bottom of 4 serving bowls. Toss the strawberries and melon balls and divide equally among the bowls, top each with a mint sprig, and serve.

## SERVES 4

# SONOMA BRAN MUFFINS

## 115
### CALORIES PER MUFFIN

We honestly think these are the best bran muffins you will ever taste. We serve them as part of the regular breakfast menu at the Sonoma Mission Inn, and they are as popular as our freshly baked croissants. The trick is to underbake the muffins, as you would chocolate chip cookies, so they stay moist. Overbaked, they become dry and tasteless.

2  cups bran flakes (miller's bran)
1/2  cup boiling water
1.  cup buttermilk
1/2  cup currants, plumped for 20 minutes in warm water, then drained
4  tablespoons (1/2 stick) unsalted butter, at room temperature
1/4  cup brown sugar
3  tablespoons blackstrap molasses
2  tablespoons mashed banana
2  eggs
1  cup stone-ground whole-wheat flour
1  tablespoon soy flour
3/4  teaspoon baking soda
1/4  teaspoon salt

Preheat the oven to 350°F. Lightly butter 12 muffin forms, dust with whole-wheat flour, and shake out the excess flour.

Put the bran in a large mixing bowl and stir in the boiling water. Add the buttermilk and currants and mix well.

With an electric mixer, cream the butter and brown sugar. With the mixer on, slowly trickle in the molasses; add the mashed banana and then the eggs, one at a time. Beat well at medium speed.

Pour the batter into the bran mixture and combine thoroughly. Add the remaining ingredients and stir until blended, but do not overmix.

Spoon the batter into the muffin tins, filling them two thirds full, and bake for 20 to 25 minutes. The muffins will look a little soft when they come out of the oven but will firm up as they cool. Serve 4 muffins for breakfast and freeze the remainder, wrapped individually in foil.

To serve the frozen muffins, simply allow them to defrost at room temperature for 2 to 3 hours or overnight. Do not reheat or the muffins will dry out.

## MAKES 12

# ARTICHOKES WITH CHICKPEA SALAD AND LEMON MAYONNAISE

## 163
### CALORIES PER SERVING

The focus of this excellent winter vegetable salad is a tender artichoke bottom filled with marinated mushrooms and chickpeas, on a bed of pretty red leaf lettuce. If you can find radicchio, the crimson and white lettucelike leaf is even more attractive. The artichokes, filling, and lemon-scented mayonnaise can all be prepared the day before.

Generous ⅓ cup dried chickpeas
1 cup sliced mushrooms
¼ cup Fresh Herb and Garlic Dressing (page 26)
Freshly ground white pepper to taste
Vegetable seasoning to taste

4 medium artichokes
1 tablespoon fresh lemon juice

## LEMON MAYONNAISE
Juice and grated rind of 1 lemon
½ cup Spa Mayonnaise (page 43)

2 cups shredded red leaf lettuce
2 carrots, peeled and cut into julienne strips
2 medium zucchini, cut into julienne strips

## GARNISH
¼ red pepper, cut into julienne strips

**TO PREPARE THE FILLING:** Put the chickpeas in a saucepan, add 6 cups of water, and bring to a boil. Reduce the heat, partially cover, and cook at a rapid simmer for 1 hour, or until the chickpeas are tender. Drain well and put in a mixing bowl. Add the mushrooms, dressing, pepper, and vegetable seasoning and toss to blend. Cover and leave at room temperature for at least 1 hour, or refrigerate overnight.

**TO PREPARE THE ARTICHOKES:** In a large pot, bring to a boil enough water to cover the artichokes. Add the artichokes and lemon juice, return to a boil, and cook until tender, 20 to 30 minutes. Remove the artichokes with a slotted spoon and place in a large bowl of cold water. (Reserve the cooking liquid for use as a soup base.)

When the artichokes are cool enough to handle, drain, cut the stems off at the base, and strip off the leaves. (To enrich the reserved soup base, add the leaves and stems to the cooking liquid and simmer for 30 minutes. Strain, cool, and freeze.) When all the leaves are stripped, including the small inner cone of sharply pointed leaves, gently scrape out the fuzzy choke with a spoon and discard. If you are cooking the artichokes in advance, wrap the hearts in plastic wrap and refrigerate.

**TO PREPARE THE MAYONNAISE:** Combine the lemon juice and rind with the mayonnaise and refrigerate, covered.

To serve, arrange the artichoke hearts on the shredded lettuce and fill with marinated chickpeas and mushrooms. Surround with the julienned vegetables, decorate with red pepper, and serve with a bowl of lemon mayonnaise.

**SERVES 4**

# WARM HONEY-GLAZED PINEAPPLE

## 70
### CALORIES PER SERVING

For dessert, ripe pineapple slices glazed with honey offer a lovely sweet-tart counterpoint.

½ fresh pineapple
2 tablespoons honey

## GARNISH
4 slices lime

Preheat the oven to 300°F.
Peel the pineapple, removing the woody "eyes," and cut out the core. Cut crosswise into 4 slices. Place the slices on a baking sheet, drizzle the honey over them, and bake for 10 minutes. Place on 4 dessert plates and garnish each with a slice of lime.

**SERVES 4**

## D I N N E R
### 799
CALORIES

SONOMA VALLEY
RED WINE SPRITZER

JACK'S CAESAR SALAD

ROSEMARY ROAST VEAL
WITH FALL VEGETABLES

SAVORY HORSERADISH
SAUCE

GRAND MARNIER
SOUFFLÉ

HERBAL TEA OR
DECAFFEINATED COFFEE

## SONOMA VALLEY RED WINE SPRITZER

### 96
CALORIES PER SERVING

Naturally, in the heart of the California wine country we make our Spa Spritzer using Sonoma Valley Cabernet Sauvignon, Pinot Noir, or Zinfandel wine. But use any claret that pleases your palate.

- 2 cups red wine
- 2 cups sparkling mineral water

Mix the wine and mineral water and pour into tall glasses.

### SERVES 4

## JACK'S CAESAR SALAD

### 154
CALORIES PER SERVING

The origins of this most famous salad of them all are in dispute. One thing is clear: it has nothing to do with the Roman emperor Julius. At least one food authority traces its origins to California. In his *Compendium of Culinary Nonsense and Trivia,** George Lang says it was called "Aviator's Salad" when created in 1927 by Caesar Cardini, proprietor of a restaurant in Tijuana, Mexico, to honor fliers at nearby Rockwell Field in San Diego, California. With its increased popularity, the spicy salad took on the family name of Caesar. No matter—it's a classic. This is how it's made at Jack's Restaurant in New York City.

If you're entertaining, or in a hurry, prepare all the ingredients ahead and assemble them at the last minute.

### DRESSING

- 1 anchovy fillet
- 1 egg
- ½ teaspoon dry mustard
  Juice of ½ lemon
- 1 garlic clove, put through a garlic press
- 1 tablespoon extra-virgin olive oil
- ⅓ cup Fresh Herb and Garlic Dressing (page 26)

- 1 slice whole-wheat bread

- 1 small head romaine lettuce
- ⅓ cup freshly grated Parmesan cheese

**TO PREPARE THE DRESSING:** Mash the anchovy fillet in a small bowl with a fork or the back of a spoon. Add the egg and beat well with a whisk. Add the mustard, lemon juice, garlic, and olive oil and whisk for 1 minute. Add the dressing and beat until smooth. Pour into a jar, cover, and refrigerate until serving time.

**TO PREPARE THE CROUTONS:** Preheat the oven to 200°F. Trim the crusts from the bread, cut into ½-inch cubes, place on a baking tray, and dry out for 3 to 5 minutes. Let cool.

To serve, wash the romaine leaves, discarding any that are wilted, and pat dry. Tear into bite-size pieces and put in a salad or mixing bowl. Just before serving, toss the salad with the dressing, sprinkle with the croutons and cheese, toss again, and serve at once on chilled salad plates.

### SERVES 4

*New York: Clarkson N. Potter, Inc., 1980.

## ROSEMARY ROAST VEAL WITH FALL VEGETABLES

### 432
CALORIES PER SERVING

Simple roast veal can be one of the most elegant entrées. Here, the tenderest loin of veal, roasted at first by itself and then with aromatic vegetables and veal stock, is served with the pan juices and a pungent horseradish sauce. The key ingredient in this recipe is the intensely flavored stock.

- 2 pounds boneless veal loin, tied
- 1 tablespoon olive oil
- 2 sprigs fresh rosemary or 1 tablespoon dried
  Freshly ground white pepper to taste
- 1 large white onion, peeled and quartered
- 4 medium carrots, peeled and cut into thirds
- 1 celery heart
- 2 medium turnips, peeled and quartered
- 4 small beets, peeled
- ½ cup Veal Stock (page 162)

Preheat the oven to 350°F.
Put the veal roast in a casserole or high-sided ovenproof pot with a lid. Pour the oil over the veal and sprinkle with the rosemary and pepper. Cover the casserole and roast the meat for 40 minutes.
Remove from the oven and place the rosemary at the bottom of the casserole, where it will perfume the vegetables and stock. Add the vegetables, pour the stock over them, cover, and return to the oven for 15 to 20 minutes, or until the vegetables are cooked to your taste.

To serve, cut the veal into slices and distribute them equally among 4 heated dinner plates. Divide the vegetables equally among the bowls and pour the pan juices over them. Serve at once with a bowl of horseradish sauce.

SERVES 4

## SAVORY HORSERADISH SAUCE

### 25
CALORIES PER SERVING

This is a tangy, fresh sauce to serve with cold poached fish or boiled beef. Fresh horseradish root is available at many greengrocers, and if you've used it even once, bottled will never do again.

- ¼ horseradish root, peeled
- ¼ cup Spa Mayonnaise (page 43)

Grate the horseradish, using a hand grater. You should have about ¼ cup horseradish. Mix with the mayonnaise, cover, and store in the refrigerator. Let the sauce come to room temperature before serving.

SERVES 4

## GRAND MARNIER SOUFFLÉ

### 92
CALORIES PER SERVING

Flavored with orange, honey, and Grand Marnier, this is an extravagant finale for a special meal. Bake soufflés in individual molds, or use a 1-quart soufflé dish.

- 3 tablespoons honey
- ¼ cup fresh orange juice
- 1 teaspoon freshly grated orange rind
- ¼ cup Grand Marnier
- 1 tablespoon arrowroot mixed with 1 tablespoon fresh orange juice
- 3 eggs, separated

Combine the honey, orange juice, rind, and Grand Marnier in a saucepan and bring to a boil. Whisk in the arrowroot mixture and return to a boil. As soon as the liquid thickens, remove from the heat and let cool for 10 minutes or so.
Preheat the oven to 400°F. Lightly butter four 3-inch soufflé molds or a 1-quart soufflé dish.
Whisk the egg yolks into the cooled mixture.
Beat the egg whites until stiff, then fold into the custard. Spoon into the prepared molds.
Bake the 3-inch soufflés for 12 minutes, the larger one for about 15 minutes. The soufflés should be puffed and golden but still soft in the center. Serve at once.

SERVES 4

# MORE MAIN COURSES

Whole-Wheat Berries and Scallions

Eggs Ranchero

Spa Pizza

Deep Green Vegetable Terrine

Stuffed Cabbage Leaves

105

## SPA PIZZA

### 253
CALORIES PER SERVING

This is a great dish for the whole family. Crisp flour tortillas are the base for our fresh-tasting pizza. The topping variations are endless: use sautéed onions, zucchini, green or red peppers, or eggplant instead of, or in addition to, the mushrooms. The pizza requires almost no advance preparation, and it can be made in minutes.

- 1 tablespoon olive oil
- ½ cup chopped onion
- 1½ cups Fresh Tomato Sauce (page 59)
- 1 teaspoon fresh oregano or ½ teaspoon dried
- 4 six-inch flour tortillas
- 1 cup grated whole-milk mozzarella
- ⅔ cup sliced mushrooms
- 12 pitted black olives, cut into small dice

Preheat the oven to 350°F.

Heat the olive oil in a small saucepan, add the onion, and sauté over medium heat for 3 to 5 minutes, until translucent. Add the sauce and oregano and cook for 1 minute. Remove from heat.

Place the tortillas on a baking sheet and put in the oven for 4 to 5 minutes to crisp them. Remove from the oven and spread each tortilla with one quarter of the tomato sauce mixture, then top with the mozzarella, mushrooms, and olives. Return to the oven for 5 minutes, or until the cheese melts. Serve at once.

SERVES 4

## DEEP GREEN VEGETABLE TERRINE

### 220
CALORIES PER SERVING

We created the solution for a number of occasions, a beautiful low-calorie vegetable terrine combining spinach and Swiss chard, eggs, ricotta, and Parmesan cheese. Serve it for dinner with Whole-Wheat Berries and Scallions. Present it on a decorative platter, hot or at room temperature, as part of an elegant buffet table; or use it as an appetizer.

- ½ pound fresh spinach
- ½ pound Swiss chard
- 2 tablespoons unsalted butter
- 1 medium red onion, minced
  Freshly ground nutmeg to taste
  Freshly ground white pepper to taste
  Vegetable seasoning to taste
- 4 eggs, beaten
- ¼ cup low-fat ricotta cheese
- ¼ cup freshly grated Parmesan cheese

GARNISH

- 2 carrots, peeled and cut into julienne strips
- 4 cherry tomatoes, halved

Preheat the oven to 350°F. Lightly butter a 6 × 4 × 4-inch baking pan, or use a nonstick pan.

Remove the stems from the spinach and chard. Wash the leaves thoroughly, pat them dry, and chop coarsely.

Melt the butter in a large skillet, add the onion, and sauté over medium-high heat for 3 to 5 minutes. Add the spinach and chard and toss for 3 minutes. Season with nutmeg, pepper, and vegetable seasoning and turn into a large mixing bowl to cool.

Add the eggs, ricotta cheese, and Parmesan cheese to the spinach mixture and blend well. Pour into the prepared baking pan and bake for 45 minutes. Remove from the oven and let stand for 10 minutes before unmolding the loaf.

To serve, cut into 4 lengthwise slices and place on heated dinner plates. Decorate with the carrots and cherry tomatoes.

SERVES 4

## EGGS RANCHERO

### 302
CALORIES PER SERVING

Easy eggs served Mexican style are a good dish for a light lunch or for spicy Sunday brunch. Cook the eggs any way you like: poached, scrambled, shirred, or gently fried in a very lightly buttered or nonstick skillet. Omitting the butter will save about 30 calories per serving.

- 4 corn tortillas
- 1 cup refried beans (page 39)
- 8 eggs
- 4 teaspoons unsalted butter (optional)
- 1 cup Piquant Tomato Salsa (page 39)

Preheat the oven to 350°F.

Place the tortillas on a baking sheet and bake for 3 to 5 minutes, until crisp.

Heat the refried beans and spread on the tortillas. If you are frying or scrambling the eggs, use 1 teaspoon of butter for each 2-egg serving, and cook in a nonstick skillet. Place 2 eggs on each tortilla, spoon ¼ cup of salsa on the side, and serve.

SERVES 4

# STUFFED CABBAGE LEAVES

## 210
### CALORIES PER SERVING

This is cabbage stuffing with a difference—sautéed onion, fluffy bulgur, sunflower seeds, raisins, and freshly grated ginger. Serve the cabbage rolls with a tossed green salad.

⅔ cup bulgur
2 teaspoons unsalted butter
1 cup chopped onion
1 garlic clove, minced
¼ cup raw sunflower seeds
¼ cup raisins
1 tablespoon grated peeled ginger
  Freshly ground white pepper to taste
  Vegetable seasoning to taste
10 large green cabbage leaves
½ cup Vegetable Broth (page 163)
¼ cup diagonally sliced scallions

Cook the bulgur in 6 cups of simmering water for 25 minutes. When tender, drain and set aside.

Melt the butter in a small saucepan, add the onion and garlic, and sauté over medium heat for 3 to 5 minutes, until translucent. Transfer to a mixing bowl, add the bulgur, sunflower seeds, raisins, ginger, and seasonings, and mix well to combine. Let the stuffing cool.

Preheat the oven to 325°F.

Blanch the cabbage leaves for 30 seconds in a large pot of boiling water. Drain and immediately plunge into a bowl of cold water. When the leaves are cool enough to handle, drain and pat dry.

Spread out 8 cabbage leaves on a work surface. Fill each leaf with an equal amount of stuffing, and roll into packages from the stem end, tucking in the sides neatly. Use the 2 remaining leaves to patch any tears. Place the rolls, seam side down, in a single layer in a baking pan just large enough to hold them, and pour the Vegetable Broth over them. Bake for 30 minutes; the cabbage leaves should be fork-tender.

Serve the cabbage rolls in heated shallow soup bowls, 2 rolls to a bowl, and pour the broth over them. Sprinkle with scallions.

**SERVES 4**

# WHOLE-WHEAT BERRIES AND SCALLIONS

## 140
### CALORIES PER SERVING

If you have never eaten them before, whole-wheat berries will be a delicious discovery. They are almost as versatile as wild rice (and a lot less expensive) and just as satisfying, with a crunchy texture and nutlike flavor. The berries, resembling brown rice, are sold loose in health-food stores and are very easy to cook. Serve them as simply or elaborately as you wish. In this recipe, we use only chopped scallions and garlic tossed in butter with diced red pepper. You could easily add sautéed diced carrots and zucchini.

1¼ cups whole-wheat berries
1½ teaspoons unsalted butter
1 garlic clove, minced
½ red pepper, diced
3 scallions, chopped

Place the berries in a 3- to 4-quart pot with 2 quarts of water. Bring to a boil, lower the heat, and cook, partially covered, at a rapid simmer for 1 hour, or until the berries are tender but still very crunchy. Check the pot occasionally to see that the water has not evaporated, and add more boiling water if necessary. Drain the berries in a strainer; you should have about 2 cups.

Melt the butter in a skillet, then add the garlic and toss for 2 minutes over medium-high heat. Remove the garlic and add the red pepper; saute for 4 or 5 minutes, then add the scallions and toss for 1 minute more. Add the drained berries, stir briefly to combine, and serve.

Wheat berries can also make a terrific salad; simply toss the drained, hot berries with Spa Vinaigrette (page 23) and let them cool to room temperature before serving. Diced red onion, peppers, and fresh herbs all make nice additions to this hearty salad.

**SERVES 4**

Spa Custard with Maple Syrup Sauce

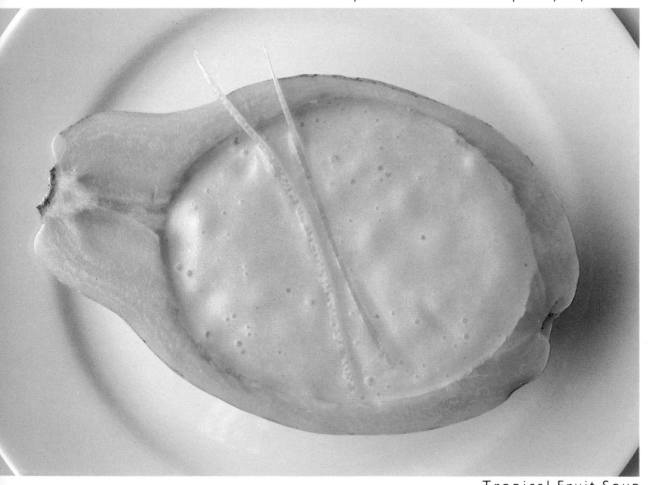

Tropical Fruit Soup

# MORE DESSERTS

Coffee-Rum Zabaglione

Honey-Vanilla Heart with Raspberry Purée

Coconut-Carob Truffles

# HONEY-VANILLA HEART WITH RASPBERRY PURÉE

## 94
### CALORIES PER SERVING

This is one of our best-known desserts, and although the preparation takes time, it is well worth undertaking for special occasions. You will need four small *coeur à la crème* molds: heart-shaped porcelain dishes about 3 inches long, 2½ inches wide, and 1½ inches deep, with holes in the bottom to allow excess liquid to drain out. The molds are available in most fine cookware stores.

- 1  vanilla bean
- 2  cups plain whole-milk yogurt
-    Pinch of barley malt sweetener
- 1  tablespoon honey
- 1  packet unflavored gelatin
- ¼  cup cold water

### GARNISH

- ½  cup raspberry purée
- 2  fresh strawberries, cut in half

The night before serving, slit the vanilla bean open lengthwise with a small sharp knife. With the tip of the knife, scrape the seeds into a mixing bowl. Add the yogurt, barley malt sweetener, and honey and mix well. Line a small bowl with a double layer of cheesecloth. Scrape the yogurt mixture into the bowl, bring up the ends of the cheesecloth, and tie securely. The yogurt must now hang free to drain overnight. Slip the shaft of a long-handled spoon under the knot and suspend the cheesecloth bag over a deep bowl, with the ends of the spoon set on the rim of the bowl. Refrigerate.

The next day, empty the yogurt mixture into a bowl, discarding the cheesecloth and the liquid that has drained off. In a small metal bowl, soften the gelatin in the water. Place the bowl over boiling water and remove as soon as the gelatin has dissolved. Rapidly blend into the yogurt mixture, stirring vigorously to distribute the gelatin evenly before it sets.

Line 4 small *coeur à la crème* molds with a single layer of cheesecloth and fill with the yogurt mixture. Place the molds on a large deep plate and refrigerate for at least 2 hours.

To serve, invert the molds onto chilled dessert plates and carefully remove the cheesecloth. Spoon 2 tablespoons of Raspberry Purée around each heart and top each with half a strawberry. Serve immediately.

**SERVES 4**

# SPA CUSTARD WITH MAPLE SYRUP SAUCE

## 213
### CALORIES PER SERVING

A variation on a French crème caramel, our all-American custard is flavored with cinnamon, nutmeg, and honey. It's especially good served with the Maple Syrup Sauce, but for a change you could substitute raspberry purée. You can bake the custard in individual ramekins or in a 1-quart soufflé dish, and save the extra servings for another meal. The custard shown in our photograph is decorated with a thin slice of unpeeled apple cut into the shape of a maple leaf, but the dessert will in no way suffer from its omission.

- 4  eggs
- 1  egg white
-    Pinch of ground cinnamon
-    Pinch of freshly ground nutmeg
-    Pinch of barley malt sweetener
- ⅓  cup honey
- 2½  cups whole milk

### MAPLE SYRUP SAUCE

- 1  egg yolk, at room temperature
- ¼  cup maple syrup
- 4  drops vanilla extract
- ¼  cup very cold nonfat skim milk

**TO PREPARE THE CUSTARD:** Preheat the oven to 300°F. Lightly butter six 3-inch custard cups or a 1-quart soufflé dish.

Mix all the custard ingredients in a blender for 30 seconds. Pour into the custard cups. Place the cups in a baking pan and pour in enough very hot tap water to reach halfway up the sides of the cups. Bake until the custard is set, 1 hour for the cups, 80 minutes for the 1-quart mold. Remove from the oven and let the custard cool to room temperature, then chill until cold, about 1 hour.

**TO PREPARE THE SAUCE:** Whisk the egg yolk in a small bowl until it is thick and lemon-colored, about 3 minutes. In a small saucepan, bring the maple syrup to a boil. Pour the boiling syrup over the egg yolk, whisking constantly. Allow the mixture to cool, then chill.

To serve, run a knife around the edge of 4 of the custards and unmold on chilled dessert plates. Put the vanilla extract and skim milk in the beaker of an immersion blender, insert the whipping nozzle, and whip the milk. Immediately fold the whipped milk into the cold maple syrup mixture and spoon the sauce around the custards.

**SERVES 6**

# TROPICAL FRUIT SOUP

## 118
### CALORIES PER SERVING

In Scandinavia, Germany, and Eastern Europe cold fruit soups are often served as a snack or for dessert. They are very easy to make, and the perfect finishing touch for a light summer meal.

- 2 medium papayas
- 1 large mango
- 1 cup unsweetened apple juice
- 1 cup nonfat skim milk
- 1 tablespoon honey
  Pinch of ground cinnamon

### GARNISH
  Thin julienne strips lemon rind

Chill all ingredients for at least an hour before preparing.

Cut the papayas in half and scoop out the seeds. Carefully remove the flesh, leaving 1/4 inch of pulp still attached to the skin. Reserve the pulp and papaya shell.

Peel and seed the mango and cut into large cubes. Add to the papaya pulp; you should have a total of about 2 cups of pulp. Put the pulp, apple juice, milk, honey, and cinnamon in a blender and purée. Pour into the papaya shells and serve at once, decorated with the lemon rind.

**SERVES 4**

# COCONUT-CAROB TRUFFLES

## 22
### CALORIES PER TRUFFLE

A special treat to serve with after-dinner coffee or as a snack, our Spa truffles will keep for 2 to 3 weeks in the refrigerator, and they also make a wonderful gift. Prebaked carob can be bought at health-food stores.

- 6 pitted dried dates
- 1/2 cup prebaked carob
- 1/4 cup unsweetened desiccated coconut
- 1/4 cup dry whole-wheat bread crumbs (made from 1 to 2 crustless slices)
- 2 tablespoons plain low-fat yogurt
- 3 tablespoons honey
- 1 teaspoon vanilla extract

Using the back of a fork, mash the dates in a bowl. Mix in 1/4 cup of the carob and the coconut. Add the bread crumbs, yogurt, honey, and vanilla extract and mix well. Cover and chill.

Spread the remaining carob powder on a sheet of wax paper. With a 3/4-inch melon-baller dipped in hot water, scoop up approximately 1 tablespoon of the truffle mixture at a time, form into 1-inch balls, and roll in carob powder. Store the truffles in the refrigerator in an airtight container, but serve them at room temperature.

**MAKES 24**

# COFFEE-RUM ZABAGLIONE

## 100
### CALORIES PER SERVING

A variation on the classic Italian dessert, this version has a subtle coffee-rum finish and a deep rich color. Eminently practical for last-minute entertaining, it is made from ingredients found in every household (so you don't need to shop) and can be whisked up in minutes. It also makes a flavorful sauce—hot or cold—to dress up any simple fruit dessert, such as poached pears, baked apples, or fresh strawberries. If used as a sauce, this recipe will serve 6. This is not for those who are on a low-cholesterol diet.

- 4 egg yolks
- 1 tablespoon dark rum
- 1 1/4 teaspoons instant coffee dissolved in 1/4 cup boiling water
- 2 tablespoons honey
  Pinch of barley malt sweetener

### GARNISH
  12 whole coffee beans (optional)

Mix all the ingredients in a stainless steel bowl or the top of a double boiler. Set over simmering water and whisk constantly for 3 to 5 minutes, or until thick and frothy. Serve at once in glass goblets, topping each serving with a few coffee beans.

**SERVES 4**

# BRIEFCASE LUNCHES

## MENU I
### 371
#### CALORIES

COLD SPICED TOMATO
SOUP

COLD HERBED PASTA
SALAD

FRESH FRUIT OR AN
OATMEAL COOKIE

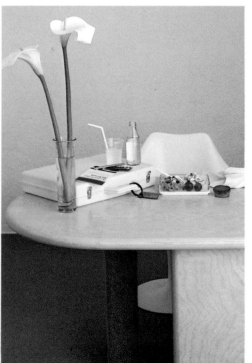

# MENU 2
## 359
### CALORIES

SWEET CARROT SALAD

SAN FRANCISCO
DEVILED CRAB

CHERRY TOMATOES

FRESH FRUIT OR A SPA
GÉNOISE

## COLD SPICED TOMATO SOUP

### 89
CALORIES PER CUP

This clear, rich soup tastes wonderful hot or cold. Good-quality imported canned plum tomatoes and Rich Chicken Stock will produce the most savory soup.

- 1 teaspoon unsalted butter
- ¼ cup diced carrot
- ¼ cup diced celery
- ¼ cup diced onion
- 1 garlic clove, minced
- 1 (1-pound 12-ounce) can imported plum tomatoes or 3 pounds fresh tomatoes
- 1 quart Rich Chicken Stock (page 161)
- 1 tablespoon chopped fresh basil or 1½ teaspoons dried
- 1 tablespoon chopped fresh parsley
- ½ teaspoon whole black peppercorns
- 1 whole clove
- 1 bay leaf
  Pinch of dried thyme
  Vegetable seasoning to taste

### GARNISH
- 1 tablespoon chopped scallion (optional)

Melt the butter in a 3½-quart pot, preferably nonstick; add the carrot, celery, onion, and garlic, and toss over medium heat for 1 minute. Add all the remaining ingredients except the scallion and bring to a boil, then lower the heat and simmer, uncovered, for 40 minutes.

Strain the soup through a fine sieve, but do not press too hard on the vegetables or the broth will become clouded. Cool and chill. Pour 1 cup of soup into a small Thermos for your Briefcase Lunch and sprinkle with the chopped scallions. Freeze the rest of the soup in convenient quantities. Don't forget to readjust the seasonings when defrosting.

**MAKES 1 QUART**

## COLD HERBED PASTA SALAD

### 204
CALORIES PER SERVING

This salad is a hearty reward if you're virtuous enough to be dining at your desk, and it's also a particularly satisfying alternative to airplane food. The combination of whole-wheat pasta and mushrooms makes a complete protein. Leftovers will find eager takers among your family, or they can be saved for another meal.

- 2 ounces whole-wheat spaghetti, broken into thirds
- 2 peeled carrots
- 2 medium zucchini
- 16 large button or fresh shiitake mushrooms, thinly sliced
- ¼ cup chopped fresh basil
- 2 recipes Fresh Herb and Garlic Dressing (page 26)

- 2 tomatoes, peeled, seeded, and cut into ¼-inch dice
- ¼ cup freshly grated Parmesan cheese

Cook the pasta in 2 quarts of rapidly boiling water.

While the pasta is cooking, put the carrots through the fine shredder of a food processor. When the pasta is al dente—tender but still firm to the bite—hold a strainer over the pot near the edge and scoop the pasta into it with a slotted spoon or wire skimmer. Do not pour off the boiling water. Set the pasta aside to drain. Toss the carrots into the boiling pasta water and blanch for 30 seconds. Drain and immediately refresh the carrots in a bowl of cold water. Drain again and let cool.

Cut off the ends of the zucchini. Hold a sharp knife at one end and cut down the length of a zucchini, removing the rind and about ¼ inch of pulp, but leaving the seeds. Repeat for the 3 remaining sides, then cut the other 3 zucchini the same way. Discard the cores (or reserve for another use) and put the 16 pieces of rind and pulp through the fine shredder of the food processor.

When the pasta and carrot are at room temperature, toss with the zucchini, mushrooms, basil, and dressing. For the Briefcase Lunch, put one quarter of the salad in a container with a tightly fitting lid. Pack one quarter of the tomatoes and Parmesan cheese in separate containers, cover, and chill. Cover the remaining salad, tomatoes, and cheese and store in the refrigerator.

**SERVES 4**

## FRESH FRUIT OR AN OATMEAL COOKIE

Pack one perfect piece of seasonal fruit per person, or an oatmeal cookie. The type and size of the fruit will, of course, affect the overall calorie total for this lunch.

# CARLENE'S OATMEAL COOKIES

## 78
### CALORIES PER COOKIE

An old-fashioned, chewy cookie, studded with raisins.

- 4 tablespoons (½ stick) unsalted butter, at room temperature
- 6 tablespoons brown sugar
- ¼ teaspoon barley malt sweetener
- 1 egg, lightly beaten
- 1 teaspoon vanilla extract
- ¼ cup stone-ground whole-wheat flour
- ½ teaspoon baking powder
- ½ cup raw wheat germ
- ¾ cup rolled oats
- ½ cup raisins

Preheat the oven to 375°F. If you do not have a nonstick baking sheet, very lightly butter a regular baking sheet.

In a mixing bowl, cream the butter, sugar, and barley malt sweetener. Add the egg and vanilla extract and blend well. Add the remaining ingredients and mix just until well blended.

Drop dough by teaspoonfuls onto the baking sheet, leaving 2 inches between each cookie. Bake for 10 to 12 minutes and let cool on racks. Store for 1 week in an airtight container, or freeze for up to 6 months.

**MAKES 18**

# SWEET CARROT SALAD

## 107
### CALORIES PER SERVING

The bright color and taste of this special salad make it the next best thing to sunshine if you're eating indoors.

- ½ cup plain low-fat yogurt
- 4 teaspoons honey
- 2 cups grated carrots
- ¼ cup raisins
- 4 teaspoons thinly sliced almonds, toasted for 5 minutes in a preheated 375°F. oven

Mix the yogurt and honey. Add the remaining ingredients, toss, and chill.

**SERVES 4**

# SAN FRANCISCO DEVILED CRAB

## 162
### CALORIES PER SERVING

A luxurious lunch to indulge in while working, fresh crab meat, hard-cooked eggs, and chopped red onion are spiced with Dijon mustard and mixed with creamy Dilled Yogurt Sauce. We prefer San Francisco Dungeness crab, the sweetest, most tender kind, but any fresh regional crab will do. Do not use canned crab meat for this recipe; it contains too much sodium. Leftover salad can be served as an appetizer or saved for another lunch.

- 12 ounces fresh crab meat, or frozen, thawed
- 2 hard-cooked eggs, chopped
- 2 teaspoons chopped parsley
- ¼ cup minced red onion
- 4 teaspoons Dijon mustard
- ½ cup Dilled Yogurt Sauce (page 42) Freshly ground white pepper to taste Vegetable seasoning to taste
- 2 lettuce leaves per serving
- 2 cherry tomatoes per serving
- 1 lemon wedge per serving

If you are using fresh lump crab meat, pick it over for shells and cartilage. Try not to shred the meat too finely. If you use frozen crab legs, cut them into small pieces. Put all the ingredients except the lettuce, tomatoes, and lemon in a bowl and mix gently so as not to shred the crab meat too finely. For the Briefcase Lunch, line a container with the lettuce, spoon in one quarter of the crab salad, top with the tomatoes and lemon wedge, cover, and chill. Store the remaining salad, tightly covered, in the refrigerator.

**SERVES 4**

# FRESH FRUIT OR A SPA GÉNOISE

Select one piece of seasonal fruit per person. If you happen to have a Spa Génoise (page 95) on hand, this makes an ideal accompaniment to the crab salad. A génoise contains 90 calories; the fruit will differ in calories, according to type and size.

SPA MENUS
FOR
SPECIAL
OCCASIONS

Social eating is often the undoing of many a dieter—even those with the best intentions. Because food is associated with love and caring, when entertaining at home we tend to think we must provide rich, elaborate dishes and calorie-laden desserts. Of course, as host, we partake as well. Similarly, thoughtful guests may worry that not eating a caloric dish their host has spent hours preparing will be interpreted as a slight to his or her culinary skills.

This needn't be so. Here, we offer you the solution to a variety of entertaining dilemmas. Because Spa food is virtuously versatile, it can not only be enjoyed by you alone at home but also shared with friends on special occasions. This chapter contains menus ranging from a cocktail party for a group to a festive vineyard lunch for friends, to a leisurely outdoor brunch or an elegant holiday dinner party for eight.

Ideal for all types of entertaining, from casual get-togethers to the most important occasions, our Spa dishes are so satisfying that your guests may be unaware that they are low-calorie. So don't hesitate to share your Spa creations, whether it's a simple meal of garlicky-sauced artichokes, a peasant-inspired bean and potato salad and cold lemon-marinated chicken to be eaten al fresco, or a more formal repast of delicate paupiettes of sole, poached in a rich fish stock, Rock Cornish hens stuffed with wild rice and fruit and glazed with port wine, elegant braised celery hearts, savory ratatouille and a show-stopping dessert of strawberries flamed with brandy and Grand Marnier. Your guests will be even more delighted once they learn your Spa secret.

Actually, all the menus in this book can be used for entertaining, simply by doubling or tripling quantities. For extra-hungry guests, it is quite easy to add calories, either by increasing portions or by garnishing an entrée with an extra vegetable, or a dessert with a sliced strawberry, a soupçon of sauce, or a *hint* of honey. For yourself, practice portion control. Learn from experience what Spa-size servings look like and simply stop there.

Because many of these dishes can be made ahead, Spa cooking for guests is practical as well. Stocks and salad dressings are improved when made ahead because flavors blend better and intensify. Even vegetables can be steamed tender crisp ahead and reheated just before serving. Our whole holiday dinner, except for the turkey, can be prepared in advance so you can enjoy your own party.

When planning a Spa dinner party, cocktails present a potential pitfall that can be avoided with a bit of finesse and wit. We all know how difficult it is not to drink at a social gathering. Part of the problem is not having anything to do with our hands. So offer your guests something to sip; offer a healthy highball of sparkling mineral water with a decorative slice of lime, instead of high-calorie alcohol. There are many different mineral waters on the market today, both sparkling and nonsparkling, so have a variety from which to choose. Or plan a lighthearted mineral water tasting. There are popular sparkling and nonsparkling waters from France, Italy, and America. If you must serve alcohol, keep it light with spritzers and citrus cocktails, half juice and half club soda, especially cooling in spring and summer.

Instead of serving caffeinated beverages to accompany dessert, offer an array of herbal teas, or "infusions" as they are commonly called in Europe, where they are served in many fine restaurants and homes. For instance, you might present a large tea tray with a variety of teas from which to choose, such as chamomile, peppermint, lemon verbena, orange-spice, and almond.

For a classic approach, one of our guests sent out formal invitations to friends for a special "black-tie" Spa dinner. The invitations were handwritten, the setting was elegant with fabulous flowers, candlelight, beautiful linen, china, and crystal, and everyone was dressed to kill. The portions were small, the drinks were nonalcoholic. Dessert and decaffeinated espresso were served in a cozy living room before the fire. Our hostess reported that guests were as animated and entertaining as if the wine were flowing freely. As this hostess proved, there is a lot that can be done to bring theater to an event. The pleasure of dining encompasses more than simply what is on the plate.

Visualize and plan your meal as a total sensory event. Take the time to appreciate all the creative aspects of entertaining: the art of cooking foods to their point of perfection; arranging them attractively on the plate; setting an inviting and festive table; making your guests feel welcome and cared for. The pleasure of good company and stimulating conversation is as important as what you are eating. Dining in an agreeable setting and sharing beautiful food with friends makes any occasion special.

Learn to regard low-calorie cooking as a challenge: see how many different foods you can serve for the fewest calories. Many luxury foods are surprisingly low in calories. Some of our favorites are oysters; fresh crab legs with lemon (a good take-along airplane lunch); asparagus; wild mushrooms; raspberries, strawberries, and blueberries; consommés (with no added salt); soufflés made with only one egg yolk; spectacular salads with many different types of lettuce, or composed salads of diced, grated, or julienned vegetables in season.

You'll notice that the calorie counts for these special menus are somewhat higher than those in the previous sections. These totals are, however, only approximate. It is unlikely that your guests will want a full serving of each dish offered (unless it is a formal, sit-down event) or that they will want equal portions of each. But even if everyone overindulges on this luxurious party fare, no one need feel guilty—it's still far less caloric than its conventional counterparts.

# BRUNCH

## MENU
### 399
CALORIES

VICHYSSOISE

BAKED OYSTERS

WILTED SPINACH AND
MUSHROOM SALAD

POPPY SEED WAFERS

ORANGE-ZINFANDEL
SORBET

HERBAL TEA OR
DECAFFEINATED COFFEE

WINE SUGGESTION:
CHAMPAGNE

## VICHYSSOISE

### 72
CALORIES PER SERVING

Famous for good reasons, vichyssoise is easy to make and excellent for a variety of occasions, served hot as well as cold. It also makes a simple presentation, with snippets of dark green chives. At the Spa we use non-fat skim milk to give it a creamier texture than our Leek and Potato Soup (page 78). As with all our soups, the essential ingredient is the stock—homemade chicken or vegetable stock—to ensure richly flavorful results.

1 teaspoon unsalted butter
3 medium leeks (white part only), chopped
1 small onion, chopped
1 large baking potato, peeled and coarsely chopped
1 quart Chicken Stock (page 161) or Vegetable Broth (page 163)
½ cup nonfat skim milk
  Freshly ground white pepper to taste
  Vegetable seasoning to taste

### GARNISH
1 tablespoon chopped fresh chives

Melt the butter over low heat in a 3-quart nonstick saucepan, add the leeks, onion, and potato, and sauté gently for 2 minutes. Do not allow the vegetables to brown. Add the stock,

bring to a boil, reduce the heat, and simmer, covered, for 20 to 30 minutes, or until the vegetables are very tender. Purée the soup in several batches in a blender or food processor, let cool, then refrigerate until cold.

Just before serving, stir in the cold skim milk. Taste the soup and season with pepper and vegetable seasoning. Pour into chilled soup bowls and decorate with the chives.

SERVES 4

## BAKED OYSTERS

### 60
CALORIES PER SERVING

Briny oysters baked in their natural juices are so perfect in themselves that they really need no embellishment other than a few drops of lemon juice. (As purists, we consider the addition of hot sauce gilding the lily, but that is a matter of taste.) Best of all, you don't have to open them—the heat of the oven does it for you. Fresh oysters are now available year round, which is when to enjoy them. There are many varieties of oysters, and every connoisseur has a favorite—Malpeques, French Belon, and Blue Points are most prized—but ask your fishmonger what's freshest, and experiment to find yours.

16 medium live oysters (in their shells)
4 lemon wedges
  Tabasco sauce or other hot sauce, to taste

Preheat the oven to 350°F.
Wash the oyster shells under cold running water and scrub off the sand with a stiff brush. Place the oysters on a baking sheet and bake

just until the shells open, about 5 minutes. Do not overcook. Transfer 4 oysters to each plate, taking care not to spill any of the juices. Lift the lids gently, but do not remove (they will help keep the oysters warm), add a lemon wedge to each plate, and serve with oyster forks. Pass the Tabasco sauce separately.

SERVES 4

## WILTED SPINACH AND MUSHROOM SALAD

### 87
CALORIES PER SERVING

In this very popular salad the spinach is not actually cooked in the hot dressing, only wilted a bit to produce a subtle contrast in texture with the mushrooms. If you have calories to burn, or thin guests, add a few finely chopped walnuts.

1 pound tender young spinach leaves
12 mushrooms
2 tablespoons minced red onion
5 tablespoons Spa Vinaigrette (page 23) made with walnut oil
1 hard-cooked egg

Remove and discard the spinach stems. Put the leaves in a sink filled with cold water and swirl them around to dislodge the sand. Put the leaves in a colander, leaving the sand at the bottom of the sink. If there is still sand on the leaves, drain and rinse out the sink and repeat the process. Shake the leaves in the colander to get off as much water as possible, then pat dry with towels.

Cut off the mushroom stems (reserve them for stock), clean the caps with a soft brush or cloth, and slice 8 of them.

Warm a large stainless steel bowl or 12-inch sauté pan over high heat, add the onion and vinaigrette, and heat for 1 minute. Remove the pan from the burner, add the spinach, egg wedges, and mushrooms, and toss to coat with the dressing. Turn into a large salad bowl, add the 4 reserved whole mushrooms, and let your guests help themselves.

SERVES 4

## POPPY SEED WAFERS

### 92
CALORIES PER WAFER

These crisp crackers are sparked with the nutlike flavor and crunch of poppy seeds. They may be made several days in advance and stored in tightly covered tins. You may also serve them as an hors d'oeuvre with spreads such as Walnut Pâté (page 91).

1½ cups stone-ground whole-wheat flour
2½ teaspoons baking powder
¼ teaspoon baking soda
½ teaspoon vegetable seasoning
4 tablespoons (½ stick) cold unsalted butter, cut into ¼-inch dice
¾ cup buttermilk
½ cup poppy seeds

Preheat the oven to 425°F.

In the bowl of an electric mixer, combine the flour, baking powder, baking soda, and vegetable seasoning. Add the butter and with the flat beater cut it into the dry ingredients until the mixture resembles cornmeal. Add the buttermilk all at once and knead at low speed with the dough hook, or by hand, until the dough is smooth, about 2 minutes.

Transfer the dough to a work surface and roll with your hands into a log 1 inch thick. Cut the log into 16 equal pieces and move to one side. Sprinkle 1½ teaspoons of poppy seeds on the counter, place 1 piece of the dough in the center, and, with a rolling pin, roll into a thin circle about 3 inches in diameter. Place on an un-greased baking sheet and continue to roll out the wafers, replenishing the poppy seeds as needed, until the baking sheet is filled. You may need two baking sheets.

Bake for 15 minutes, until lightly browned, remove from the baking sheet with a spatula, and let cool on racks.

MAKES 16 WAFERS

## ORANGE-ZINFANDEL SORBET

### 88
CALORIES PER SERVING

A uniquely American dessert, this sorbet gets its color and flavor from Zinfandel, the robust red wine made from grapes grown only in California. It was originally created for the dinner menu of the Provençal Grill, the res-taurant at the Sonoma Mission Inn. Do not strain the orange juice once you have squeezed it; the small pieces of pulp make the texture more in-teresting.

1 cup red Zinfandel
1 cup fresh orange juice, with pulp
1 cup water
1 tablespoon grated orange rind
2 to 3 teaspoons barley malt sweetener

If you have an electric or hand-powered ice cream maker, combine all the ingredients and follow the man-ufacturer's instructions for making sherbet. To make the sorbet in the freezer, put all the ingredients in a metal bowl, place in the freezer, and leave until frozen solid. Remove the bowl from the freezer and break the sorbet into large chunks with a fork. Purée the chunks in a food processor until smooth and creamy. Return to the bowl and freeze for 30 minutes.

Serve in chilled wineglasses.

SERVES 4

# BARBECUE

## MENU

### 828
CALORIES

SKEWERED SHRIMP AND SEA SCALLOPS
WITH EGGPLANT AND PEPPERS

LOIN OF VEAL WITH
POMEGRANATE JUICE MARINADE

PINTO BEAN CHILI

ARUGULA, ROMAINE, AND
RED LEAF LETTUCE SALAD

SUNSET SPRITZER

WATERMELON

ICED ALMOND TEA

# SKEWERED SHRIMP AND SEA SCALLOPS WITH EGGPLANT AND PEPPERS

## 164
### CALORIES PER SERVING

For a festive summer barbecue, we start with a grill of skewered seafood, peppers, and eggplant that can be prepared several hours in advance. Do not marinate this dish; the slight acidity of the sauce would make the shrimp mushy. The seafood and vegetables are threaded separately on metal skewers so that each can be cooked for the perfect length of time. Keep the skewers away from the center of the grill, where the intense heat could burn the food before it was cooked through. The barbecue sauce is 44 calories per ¼ cup.

    24  large shrimps, peeled
    24  sea scallops
     1  red and 1 green pepper
     1  medium unpeeled eggplant

### BARBECUE SAUCE
    ¼  cup minced onion
     2  garlic cloves, minced
     2  cups tomato purée
    ½  cup rice vinegar
    ½  cup water
     3  tablespoons honey
    ¼  teaspoon Tabasco sauce or other
        hot sauce
        Pinch of vegetable seasoning

Thread the shrimps and scallops separately onto skewers. Remove the stems from the peppers, cut them into quarters, remove the seeds, and cut away the white membranes. Cut each quarter in half. Cut the eggplant into 2-inch cubes. Thread the peppers and eggplant together on skewers.

Mix all the sauce ingredients in a bowl and refrigerate, covered, until ready to use. Just before putting them on the grill, brush the filled skewers on all sides with Barbecue Sauce, and continue to baste them while they cook.

Grill the peppers and eggplant for 10 to 12 minutes, keeping the skewers well away from the center of the grill. Watch the eggplant carefully to see that it does not overcook and fall off the skewers. Turn often. Grill the shrimps and scallops for 6 to 8 minutes, turning often.

**SERVES 8**

# LOIN OF VEAL WITH POMEGRANATE JUICE MARINADE

## 226
### CALORIES PER SERVING

In the Middle East pomegranate juice and fresh coriander are traditional ingredients for marinating lamb and other meats. Bottled pomegranate juice can be bought in health-food stores. It has a slightly sweet, slightly pungent taste. Serve leftovers cold, with a mustardy mayonnaise, or toss julienned strips into a chef's salad.

### MARINADE
     2  cups unsweetened pomegranate
        juice
    ½  cup red wine vinegar
     1  medium onion, quartered
     2  garlic cloves
     2  tablespoons honey
     1  tablespoon fresh lemon juice

     1  bunch fresh coriander (cilantro)
     3  pounds boneless loin or leg of veal,
        tied

Combine all the marinade ingredients in a blender or food processor and purée.

Spread the coriander (including stems) over the loin of veal and press into the meat. Put the veal in a bowl just large enough to hold it comfortably. Pour the marinade over the meat and let stand at room temperature for 4 hours, turning often, or leave overnight in the refrigerator, turning as often as you can. Pat the coriander leaves back on the veal if they fall off as you turn the meat.

If the veal has marinated in the refrigerator, let it come to room temperature before you grill it. Scrape off the coriander leaves and grill the veal for about 1 hour, turning it every 10 minutes so that it cooks evenly. To prevent burning, keep the meat near the edge of the fire, not directly over it, and baste with the marinade.

The roast will be ready when the internal temperature is 165°F. (Use an instant-reading meat thermometer.) Allow the veal to rest for 15 minutes, then cut into thin slices and serve.

**NOTE:** Here's the way a chef tests roasted meat to see whether it is rare, medium, or well done: Plunge a metal skewer all the way through the center of the meat and leave it there for 15 seconds. Withdraw the skewer and immediately touch the middle of it to your lower lip. If the skewer is hot, the meat is well done; if it is warm, the meat is medium rare; and if the skewer is cold, the meat is rare.

**SERVES 12**

## PINTO BEAN CHILI

### 156
CALORIES PER SERVING

One of our most flavorful dishes, Pinto Bean Chili is always a hit. This chili tastes so good, we have written a double recipe. Freeze 1 quart to have on hand for another party. We recommend cooking the dried pinto beans from scratch (they need very little attention) and using imported canned plum tomatoes if fresh tomatoes are not at their peak. The bottled salsa available in health food stores, which is free of additives, is an acceptable substitute for homemade.

3 cups dried pinto beans
2 tablespoons olive oil
1 large white onion, minced
3 garlic cloves, put through a garlic press
1 red pepper, stemmed, seeded, and cut into ¼-inch dice
2 cups unpeeled tomatoes, seeded and diced, or imported canned plum tomatoes
3 bay leaves
2 tablespoons chili powder
2 tablespoons dried oregano
2 teaspoons ground cumin
1 cup Piquant Tomato Salsa (page 39) or bottled salsa

Soak the pinto beans overnight in cold water to cover. The next day, drain the beans, cover with 4 quarts of cold water, and bring to a boil. Lower the heat and cook the beans gently, uncovered, until tender, about 70 to 80 minutes. Drain beans. (You should have about 6 cups of cooked beans.)

In a 3- to 4-quart saucepan, heat the olive oil, add the onion, garlic, and pepper, and sauté over medium heat for 3 to 5 minutes, until translucent. Add the beans and all remaining ingredients except the salsa. Bring to a boil, lower the heat, and simmer, uncovered, for 30 minutes.

Serve the chili hot or at room temperature, with a bowl of salsa on the side. If you like your chili very hot, add Tabasco or other hot sauce, chopped jalapeño peppers, or more chili powder to taste.

**MAKES 16 SERVINGS**

## ARUGULA, ROMAINE, AND RED LEAF LETTUCE SALAD

### 112
CALORIES PER SERVING

Arugula, or rocket, as it is called in the West, is a member of the mustard family. Its pungent flavor provides the salad with the strength of character lacking in the blander romaine and red leaf lettuces. If arugula is not available, use watercress. For a more colorful effect, substitute ruby-red radicchio for the red leaf lettuce. Also, remember that salad dressing is always better when prepared ahead. Substitute extra-virgin olive oil for the walnut oil if you prefer.

2 bunches arugula
1 large head romaine lettuce
1 large head red leaf lettuce
2 recipes Spa Vinaigrette (page 23) made with walnut oil

Wasn all the lettuces well in several changes of water; arugula is particularly sandy. Pat the leaves dry, tear into bite-size pieces, and place in a large salad bowl. If prepared ahead, wrap in a towel and keep refrigerated to crisp the lettuces. Just before serving, toss with the vinaigrette.

**SERVES 8**

## SUNSET SPRITZER

### 20
CALORIES PER SERVING

This sweet, nonalcoholic Spa spritzer is the color of a spectacular sunset, which is exactly when you should serve it. We like the thickness of unstrained strawberry purée, but you can make a smoother spritzer by passing the puréed strawberries through a fine sieve.

3 cups freshly squeezed orange juice
1 cup strawberry purée (about 1½ cups whole strawberries)
1 cup sparkling mineral water, chilled
Ice cubes

Mix the orange juice and strawberry purée and chill. Just before serving, add the mineral water and pour over ice cubes in tall glasses.

**SERVES 8**

## WATERMELON

### 150
CALORIES PER SERVING

No outdoor barbecue seems complete without watermelon, and a good-sized slice has only 150 calories. Keep the melon chilled until you are ready to serve it. Almost like slicing a wedding cake, cutting into a juicy watermelon in front of your guests always adds a bit of drama.

# PICNIC

# MENU
## 801
### CALORIES

ARTICHOKES WITH AÏOLI

ITALIAN SALAD

DILLED POTATO AND
BEAN SALAD

COLD LEMON-GARLIC CHICKEN

FRESH FRUITS

WATERMELON-LIME
COOLER

# ARTICHOKES WITH AÏOLI

## 138
### CALORIES PER SERVING

Eating artichokes is a leisurely pursuit, just the right thing for a picnic. The artichokes are served with aïoli, the famous garlic mayonnaise that is also called "Provençal butter." One and a half tablespoons of aïoli is about 16 calories.

### AÏOLI
½ garlic clove
¾ cup Spa Mayonnaise (page 43)

4 medium artichokes
1 lemon, halved
1 teaspoon vegetable seasoning

Put the garlic through a garlic press and mix it with the mayonnaise to make the aïoli.

Bring 4 quarts of water to a boil in a large pot. Cut off and discard the artichoke stems and rub the cut parts with lemon. Squeeze the juice from both lemon halves into the water and add the vegetable seasoning. When the water comes to a boil, add the artichokes and boil, uncovered, for 25 to 30 minutes, or until the heart feels soft when it is pierced with a knife. Start checking when the artichokes have cooked for 15 minutes.

Have a large bowl of cold water ready. When the artichokes are done, remove them from the boiling water and plunge into the cold water. Let cool in the water, then drain upside down and dry with a towel.

Carefully spread apart the leaves of each artichoke to expose the choke. With your fingers, pull out and discard the small cone of light green leaves. Using a spoon, scrape off and discard the hairy cushion, or choke. The artichokes are now ready to eat.

Serve with a small bowl of aïoli.

SERVES 4

# ITALIAN SALAD

## 159
### CALORIES PER SERVING

This is a refreshing, juicy salad especially good for warm weather. It's wonderful by itself with its fragrant basil vinaigrette or as a filling for small whole-wheat pita breads. The quality of the tomatoes and cheese is key, so buy the best vine-ripened tomatoes you can find and fresh, unsalted mozzarella, which can usually be found in Italian salumerias (delicatessens). Once you've eaten fresh mozzarella, you'll never go back to the packaged kind.

1 large cucumber
2 large ripe tomatoes, sliced
2 scallions with tops, sliced
4 ounces mozzarella cheese, cut into ¼-inch dice
½ cup Spa Vinaigrette (page 23), made with extra-virgin olive oil
2 tablespoons chopped fresh basil
Freshly ground white pepper to taste
Vegetable seasoning to taste

Peel the cucumber and cut in half lengthwise. Scrape out the seeds with a spoon and slice the cucumber into thin semicircles. In a bowl, combine the cucumbers with all the remaining ingredients and toss lightly.

SERVES 4

# DILLED POTATO AND BEAN SALAD

## 152
### CALORIES PER SERVING

This is a wonderful herb-flavored potato salad, with the added crunch of celery and the zip of minced red onion. The salad should be made the same day you serve it, to preserve the textures and flavors.

½ cup dried white beans
4 small red potatoes, scrubbed
1 hard-cooked egg, chopped
2 tablespoons minced red onion
½ celery stalk, minced
⅔ cup Spa Mayonnaise (page 43)
½ teaspoon Dijon mustard
1 teaspoon chopped fresh dill
Freshly ground white pepper to taste
Vegetable seasoning to taste

Cover the white beans with cold water and let stand overnight at room temperature. Drain the beans and put in a 2-quart pot. Add 6 cups of cold water, bring to a boil, lower the heat, and simmer, uncovered, for 1½ to 2 hours, or until tender but not mushy. Begin tasting for doneness after the beans have cooked for 1 hour and 15 minutes. Drain in a colander and rinse under cold running water, then drain again and let cool.

While the beans are cooking, put the potatoes in a small saucepan with cold water to cover. Set over high heat and bring to a boil. Cook at a fast simmer for 15 to 20 minutes, or until fork-tender. Drain the potatoes, let cool (do not peel), and cut into ¼-inch dice.

In a large mixing bowl, combine the beans, potatoes, and remaining ingredients. Toss to mix well, then chill in the refrigerator.

SERVES 4

## COLD LEMON-GARLIC CHICKEN

### 180
CALORIES PER SERVING

Chicken is the classic cold picnic dish. Here we've improved the character of broiled chicken with an aromatic lemon-garlic marinade, laden with fresh herbs. We use lemon thyme available locally, but any fresh thyme, will enhance this recipe, as will fresh tarragon or rosemary. This dish is so simple and so good, you will want to try it hot as well, when you're not dining outdoors.

If there are any leftovers, a cold breast of herbed lemon-garlic chicken is a good candidate for a Briefcase Lunch with a salad of cold asparagus tips and a few cherry tomatoes. Or, tossed with fresh greens, this flavorful chicken could be the centerpiece of a luncheon salad.

4  boneless chicken breasts halves (approximately 6 ounces each)
1  garlic clove, crushed with a knife
   Juice of 1 lemon
2  tablespoons cold-pressed vegetable oil
   Fresh or dried thyme to taste
   Freshly ground pepper to taste
   Vegetable seasoning to taste

Put all the ingredients in a bowl and toss to combine. Cover and refrigerate for 2 hours.

Preheat the broiler.

Remove the chicken breasts from the marinade and dry with paper towels. Broil for 4 to 5 minutes on each side, or until cooked but not dry. Let cool, cover well with plastic wrap or foil, and refrigerate until you pack the picnic lunch.

SERVES 4

## FRESH FRUITS

Buy a variety of the ripest seasonal fruits on the market. Grapes and cherries are high in sugar and are not included on the Spa menus. For our lunch, we chose apples, small melon halves, strawberries, and nectarines. We allowed 1 or 2 pieces for each person, approximately 80 calories.

## WATERMELON-LIME COOLER

### 92
CALORIES PER SERVING

This sweet-sour iced drink is a cooling and colorful finale to a glorious garlic-scented picnic. Lime juice cuts the sweetness of the watermelon. Serve it over mineral-water ice cubes and you've got a homemade soft drink.

¼  small watermelon
   Juice of 2 limes
   Ice cubes (preferably made from mineral water)

Remove the watermelon rind, cut the fruit into chunks, and liquefy. If you are using an electric juicer, the seeds will be strained out automatically. If you are using a blender or food processor, blend or process the watermelon, in several batches, just long enough to purée the fruit but not to pulverize the seeds; strain the watermelon purée through a coarse sieve.

Mix watermelon with the lime juice. Serve over ice cubes.

SERVES 4

# VINEYARD LUNCH

## M E N U
### 823
CALORIES

HOT BORSCHT

THREE-BEAN SALAD
WITH FRESH CORIANDER

CALIFORNIA BROCCOLI
SALAD WITH LEMON-
MUSTARD DRESSING

HERB-FLECKED FISH
TERRINE

PEANUT BUTTER COOKIES

WINE SUGGESTION:
BLANC DE PINOT NOIR

# HOT BORSCHT

## 118
CALORIES PER SERVING

In Russia there are as many different recipes for this beet soup as there are cooks, so our culinary license is in keeping with tradition.

- ½ potato, peeled and cut into ½-inch dice
- 3 to 4 beets, peeled and cut into ½-inch dice
- 6 cups Chicken Stock (page 161)
- 2 tablespoons unsalted butter
- ½ onion, chopped
- 1 celery stalk, cut into ¼-inch slices
- 1 cup chopped white cabbage
- 1 carrot, peeled and cut into ¼-inch dice
- 2 teaspoons chopped fresh dill or dill sprigs
- ¼ cup plain low-fat yogurt
  Freshly ground white pepper to taste
  Vegetable seasoning to taste

Put the potatoes, beets, and stock in a saucepan and bring to a boil. Lower the heat and cook, covered, at a rapid simmer until the vegetables are tender, about 10 to 12 minutes. Strain, reserving the broth and vegetables separately.

In the same saucepan, melt the butter, add the onion, and sauté over medium heat for 3 minutes, until translucent. Add the celery, cabbage, carrots, and reserved broth and bring to a boil. Lower the heat and simmer, covered, for 20 minutes, or until the vegetables are tender. Add the beets and potato and cook just long enough to reheat them. Pour into a Thermos that has been rinsed out with boiling water. (Soup can be made ahead and reheated.)

To serve, pour the soup into 4 soup bowls and sprinkle with dill. Pass a small bowl of yogurt, a grinder filled with white peppercorns, and a container of vegetable seasoning.

SERVES 4

# THREE-BEAN SALAD WITH FRESH CORIANDER

## 208
CALORIES PER SERVING

This salad tastes best made with freshly cooked dried beans. Prepare the salad at least 2 hours before serving, to allow the flavors to blend. This is a double recipe; reserve half for another meal.

- ½ cup dried white (navy or Great Northern) beans
- ½ cup dried pinto beans
- ½ cup dried lima beans
- ¼ cup minced red onion
- 1 garlic clove, minced
- 1 hard-cooked egg, chopped
- 1 tablespoon chopped Italian parsley
- 2 tablespoons chopped fresh coriander (cilantro), basil, or dill
- 1 cup Dilled Yogurt Sauce (page 42)
- 1 tablespoon Dijon or grainy mustard
- 2 tablespoons extra-virgin olive oil
  Freshly ground white pepper to taste
  Vegetable seasoning to taste

In separate pots, soak the white, pinto, and lima beans overnight in cold water to cover. The next day, drain the beans, return to the pots, and cover with cold water by 2 inches. Cover, bring to a boil, lower the heat, and simmer gently until tender: 50 to

60 minutes for the white beans, 70 to 80 minutes for the pinto and lima beans. Drain the cooked beans and let cool to room temperature.

Put the beans, onion, garlic, egg, and herbs in a mixing bowl.

In a small bowl, combine the Dilled Yogurt Sauce, mustard, olive oil, pepper, and vegetable seasoning and blend well. Pour over the beans and toss to coat. Cover with plastic wrap and leave for 2 hours at room temperature before serving.

MAKES 8 SERVINGS

# CALIFORNIA BROCCOLI SALAD WITH LEMON-MUSTARD DRESSING

## 134
CALORIES PER SERVING

The tangy dressing on this brightly colored dish is equally good on any cold vegetable and will keep for a week, tightly covered, in the refrigerator. Cook the vegetables on the day you plan to serve them and do not chill; they taste best at room temperature.

### LEMON MUSTARD DRESSING
- 2 tablespoons fresh lemon juice
- 2 tablespoons sparkling mineral water
- 2 tablespoons almond oil
- 1 tablespoon rice wine vinegar
- 2 tablespoons grainy mustard
- 1 tablespoon chopped chives
  Freshly ground white pepper to taste
  Vegetable seasoning to taste

1 large bunch broccoli
2 carrots, peeled and cut into julienne strips
1 small celery root, peeled and cut into julienne strips
1 medium turnip, peeled and cut into julienne strips
8 large leaves Boston lettuce

Mix the dressing ingredients in a small bowl until blended. Set aside.

Wash the broccoli, cut off the florets, and place them in a steamer basket. Remove the bottoms of the stalks and, with a paring knife, cut off the green peel and stringy fibers, to leave only the tender white flesh. Cut the peeled stalk into ½-inch slices and strew them over the florets. Steam the broccoli over boiling water for 3 to 5 minutes, to your taste. Have a bowl of cold water ready. When the broccoli is done, plunge it immediately into the cold water to stop the cooking and preserve the color.

Place the julienned vegetables in the steamer basket and steam for only 1 minute, then refresh in a separate bowl of cold water.

Drain the vegetables and pat them dry. Place the broccoli in the center of a large round serving plate. Arrange the lettuce leaves around the broccoli and fill each with the mixed julienned vegetables. Serve with a bowl of Lemon-Mustard Dressing.

SERVES 4

# HERB-FLECKED FISH TERRINE

## 311
### CALORIES PER SERVING

This is an easy and elegant party pâté, best when prepared a day in advance and made with fresh herbs. If fresh tarragon and basil are unavailable, substitute a teaspoon of dried tarragon or dill. Salmon is very caloric; use it sparingly. This recipe makes a wonderful first course and will serve 8 as an appetizer.

8 ounces sole or flounder fillets
8 ounces scallops
3 egg whites beaten lightly with a fork
½ cup heavy cream
1 pound in all diced raw shrimps, lobster, salmon, or crab meat (choose two or more)
1 tablespoon each chopped fresh chives, Italian parsley, tarragon, and basil
⅛ teaspoon freshly grated nutmeg
Freshly ground white pepper to taste
Vegetable seasoning to taste

### GARNISH

1 lemon, cut into 4 wedges
4 large leaves Boston lettuce

Before beginning, everything must be cold, so chill the processor bowl and blade, and an extra bowl, and be sure the mousse ingredients are cold.

Preheat the oven to 225°F. Lightly butter a 6-inch loaf pan, or use a nonstick pan.

Put the sole and scallops in the food processor bowl and purée for 40 seconds with the steel blade. With the motor running, slowly add the egg whites; this should take 30 seconds. Then very slowly (over the course of 1 minute) add the cream. Transfer this mixture to a clean chilled bowl and stir in the diced fish and shellfish, herbs, and seasonings. Blend well. Pour into the loaf pan, cover tightly with foil, and place in a slightly larger shallow pan. Pour enough very hot tap water into the larger pan to come halfway up the sides of the loaf pan.

Bake the terrine for 1 hour. Let cool completely to room temperature, then chill.

To serve, unmold the pâté and cut lengthwise into 4 slices. Place a lettuce leaf on each lunch plate, top with a slice of pâté, and garnish with a lemon wedge.

SERVES 4

# PEANUT BUTTER COOKIES

## 52
### CALORIES PER COOKIE

We use low-sodium peanut butter for these cookies.

1 egg
¼ cup honey
2 teaspoons molasses
½ cup chunky peanut butter
½ cup stone-ground whole-wheat flour
¼ cup raw wheat germ
½ teaspoon baking soda

Preheat the oven to 375°F. Lightly butter two cookie sheets, or use nonstick baking sheets.

In a mixing bowl, beat the egg, add the honey and molasses, and stir to combine. Stir in the peanut butter, then add the remaining ingredients and blend well. Roll small pieces of the dough into 1-inch balls and place 2 inches apart on the baking sheets. Press the balls lightly with the bottom of a glass to flatten a bit.

Bake for 12 minutes, or until golden brown. Let cool on racks. Store in tightly covered tins, or freeze for 4 to 6 months.

MAKES 30

# BUFFET DINNER

## MENU
### 839
#### CALORIES

COLD PAUPIETTES OF SOLE
WITH HERB MAYONNAISE

ROCK CORNISH HENS WITH WILD RICE
STUFFING AND PORT WINE SAUCE

BRAISED CELERY HEARTS

WATERCRESS AND ENDIVE SALAD

MONAGASQUE RATATOUILLE

FLAMED STRAWBERRIES

HERBAL TEA OR DECAFFEINATED COFFEE

WINE SUGGESTION:
CALIFORNIA CHARDONNAY

# COLD PAUPIETTES OF SOLE WITH HERB MAYONNAISE

## 76
### CALORIES PER SERVING

These are equally delicious hot or cold, as an appetizer or entrée. When you prepare the mushrooms, wash and reserve the trimmings for the game hens' Port Wine Sauce and freeze the extra stock for another use.

    1   tablespoon unsalted butter
    3   tablespoons minced shallots
    16  large mushrooms, sliced
    4   (4-ounce) fillets of sole
        Freshly ground white pepper to
        taste
        Vegetable seasoning to taste
    2   cups Fish Stock (page 160)
    8   lemon wedges

### GARNISH

    8   sprigs of parsley

    1   recipe Spa Mayonnaise (page 43)
        mixed with 4 teaspoons each
        chopped fresh chives and tarragon
        and 1 tablespoon chopped fresh
        dill.

Preheat the oven to 350°F.
Melt the butter in a nonstick sauté pan over medium heat, add the shallots, and cook for 1 minute. Add the mushrooms and toss for 1 minute more. Remove from the heat and let cool.

With a sharp knife, cut each sole fillet into 2 pieces along the length, following the seam. Season the fish with white pepper and vegetable seasoning. When the sautéed vegetables are cool, spoon them over the sole pieces. Roll up the paupiettes, beginning at the thick end. Secure the rolls with toothpicks and place in a shallow bak-

ing pan just large enough to hold them in a single layer.

Heat the stock, pour it over the fish, and bake for 3 to 5 minutes. Begin to check after 3 minutes to see if the rolls are cooked on the inside: very gently insert a toothpick or the tip of a small sharp knife into the paupiette and carefully make a small opening. If the flesh is milky white, the fish is cooked. When they are done, remove the rolls from the pan with a slotted spatula, let cool, cover, and refrigerate until cold.

To serve, place the fillets on a serving platter, surround with lemon wedges, and garnish with parsley. Pass the herb mayonnaise in a bowl.

### SERVES 8

# ROCK CORNISH HENS WITH WILD RICE STUFFING AND PORT WINE SAUCE

## 517
### CALORIES PER SERVING

Tender Cornish game hens stuffed with wild rice and raisins and served with rich Port Wine Sauce are the centerpiece for this feast. The hens may be stuffed and trussed several hours before roasting. Serve each half hen with a simple watercress and endive salad lightly dressed with walnutty Spa Vinaigrette (page 23).

    ½   cup cooked wild rice
    ¼   cup minced onion
    2   tablespoons raisins, plumped in ½
        cup warm water for 1 hour and
        drained
    4   (1½-pound) Rock Cornish game
        hens

### PORT WINE SAUCE
    1½  cups Veal Mushroom Sauce (page
        163) made with a single reduction
        of veal stock
    2   tablespoons Port wine

**TO PREPARE THE HENS:** Preheat the oven to 350°F. Combine the wild rice, onion, and raisins and stuff each hen with one quarter of the mixture. Sew up the cavities, truss the birds, and place on a rack in a roasting pan. Roast for about 1 hour, or until the leg bone moves easily in the hip socket.

Remove the birds to a platter, cover with foil, and allow to rest in a warm place while you prepare the sauce.

**TO PREPARE THE SAUCE:** Pour all the fat out of the roasting pan and add the veal sauce and wine. Bring to a boil, stirring and scraping the bottom of the pan with a wooden spoon to loosen all the browned bits. Cook over high heat until the liquid is reduced to 1 cup. Keep warm.

To serve, cut the birds in half, using poultry shears or a sharp knife. Remove as many cavity bones as possible and pull out the trussing strings. Spoon the stuffing into a serving bowl and keep warm. Place the birds on a serving platter and return to the oven for 2 to 3 minutes to reheat, then pour the sauce over the hens and bring to the table.

### SERVES 8

## BRAISED CELERY HEARTS

### 19
CALORIES PER SERVING

Most people think of celery as a raw vegetable, but the tender hearts braised in chicken stock are excellent served with poultry and game.

2 large celery hearts
Freshly ground white pepper to taste
Vegetable seasoning to taste
2 cups Chicken Stock (page 161)
2 tablespoons grated Parmesan cheese

Preheat the oven to 350°F.
Cut the celery hearts into quarters and blanch for 4 minutes in 1 quart of boiling water. Drain the hearts and place in a gratin dish just large enough to hold them in a single layer. Season with white pepper and vegetable seasoning, pour the stock over the celery, cover the pan with foil, and bake for 8 to 10 minutes. Remove the foil, sprinkle the celery with Parmesan cheese, and place under the broiler for a minute or so, until the cheese is golden brown.

With a slotted spoon, transfer the celery to a heated serving dish. (The stock remaining can be used as a base for soup.)

SERVES 8

## WATERCRESS AND ENDIVE SALAD

### 58
CALORIES PER SERVING

See Variation, page 67.

## MONAGASQUE RATATOUILLE

### 82
CALORIES PER SERVING

This distinctive recipe from the California Terrace, in Monaco, uses very little olive oil—just enough to impart the flavor, but not the calories, of Provençal cuisine. Second—and this is a radical departure from the standard recipes—the eggplant, zucchini, onion, peppers, and tomatoes all cook together and for only 5 minutes, so that each vegetable retains its characteristic flavor and texture. Serve it hot or cold.

1 small eggplant
1 zucchini
½ large onion
½ red pepper
½ green pepper
2 tablespoons extra-virgin olive oil
1 garlic clove, minced
2 cups drained imported canned plum tomatoes or 5 or 6 fresh tomatoes, peeled, seeded, and chopped
1 cup Fresh Tomato Sauce (page 59), made without basil
1 bay leaf
Pinch of fresh or dried thyme
Vegetable seasoning to taste

Cut the eggplant, zucchini, onion, and peppers into 1-inch cubes. Pour the olive oil into a large sauté pan, add the onion and garlic, and sauté over medium heat for 2 minutes. Add all the remaining ingredients and stir gently to combine; take care not to crush the vegetables. Bring to a boil, lower the heat, and simmer, uncovered, for 5 minutes. Remove the bay leaf and serve.

If you have prepared it in advance and wish to serve it hot, reheat over a medium flame, stirring the vegetables carefully from the bottom.

SERVES 8

## FLAMED STRAWBERRIES

### 87
CALORIES PER SERVING

A spectacular finish to a gala meal—ripe strawberries scented with Grand Marnier and orange rind, flamed with brandy. This dessert is worth waiting for. Have the table cleared, the dessert cups ready, and your guests alerted to the drama about to unfold. If you don't have a chafing dish, the strawberries can be heated in a pretty skillet, then quickly brought from the kitchen and flamed at the table.

2 tablespoons honey
2 tablespoons unsalted butter
1 tablespoon Grand Marnier
1 teaspoon grated orange rind
1 tablespoon water
3 cups ripe strawberries, hulled and cut in half
1 tablespoon warmed brandy

In a chafing dish or presentable skillet, mix the honey, butter, Grand Marnier, orange rind, and water. Bring to a boil and add the strawberries. Toss for 30 seconds, then sprinkle with the warmed brandy and light with a match (stand back from the pan as soon as you apply the flame). Spoon the burning liquid over the berries until the flame dies out. Serve at once, spooning into individual dessert dishes.

SERVES 8

# COCKTAIL PARTY

## MENU
### 398
#### CALORIES

YELLOW AND GREEN VEGETABLES
WITH HUMMUS DIP

CHERRY TOMATOES FILLED
WITH CRISP DICED VEGETABLES

CELERY STUFFED WITH HERBED CHEESE

SWISS CHARD AND GRUYÈRE SPREAD

SCALLOP SEVICHE ON CUCUMBER ROUNDS

SALMON AND TUNA SASHIMI

# YELLOW AND GREEN VEGETABLES WITH HUMMUS DIP

## 92
### CALORIES PER SERVING

Make this thick creamy dip ahead of time, even the night before the party, to give the flavors time to blend. Use any seasonal vegetables that strike your fancy; carrots, blanched green beans, celery, and endive are good choices.

### HUMMUS DIP

- 1 cup cooked chickpeas
- ¼ cup soft tofu
- 1 large garlic clove
- 2 tablespoons extra-virgin olive oil
- 2 tablespoons chopped Italian parsley
- ¼ cup minced scallions
  Freshly ground white pepper to taste
  Vegetable seasoning to taste

- 16 slender asparagus spears, tough ends trimmed
- 24 snow peas, ends trimmed and strings removed
- 8 broccoli florets
- 2 yellow bell peppers
- ½ pound zucchini

Purée the chickpeas, tofu, garlic, and oil in a food processor. Scrape into a bowl, add all the remaining dip ingredients, and stir to combine. Cover and store in the refrigerator for at least 2 hours before serving.

Bring a large pot of water to a boil; prepare a large bowl of cold water. Blanch the asparagus in the boiling water for 30 seconds. With tongs or a large skimmer, remove from the pot and place in the cold water. Put the snow peas in a strainer, dip into the boiling water for 10 seconds, then remove and add to the asparagus. Add the broccoli to the boiling water, cook for 30 seconds, and drain, discarding the water. Add the broccoli to the bowl of cold water. When the vegetables have cooled completely, drain and pat dry.

Remove and discard the stem from the pepper, cut it into quarters, and cut away the seeds and membranes. Cut the quarters in half lengthwise. Scrub the zucchini, cut off the ends, and cut sticks about 2½ inches long by ¼ inch thick.

Arrange the vegetables on a tray or platter and serve with the bowl of hummus.

### SERVES 8

# CHERRY TOMATOES FILLED WITH CRISP DICED VEGETABLES

## 19
### CALORIES PER SERVING

Bright red cherry tomatoes are a colorful accent for any cocktail party tray.

- 16 firm cherry tomatoes
- 1 small carrot, peeled
- 2 scallions
- 1 medium zucchini
- 1 celery stalk
- ¼ cup Fresh Herb and Garlic Dressing (page 26)

Wash the tomatoes and pat dry. Cut off the top third of each tomato and gently scrape out the seeds with a small spoon.

Cut all the vegetables into very fine dice—less than ¼ inch, if possible. Put the vegetables in a bowl, toss with the dressing, and carefully fill the tomatoes. Refrigerate until serving time. Arrange on a platter with the stuffed celery.

### SERVES 8

# CELERY STUFFED WITH HERBED CHEESE

## 54
### CALORIES PER SERVING

Crisp celery stalks are filled with a creamy blend of ricotta cheese, tangy coriander, fresh basil, and chives.

- 16 tender celery stalks, leaves on
- 1 cup low-fat ricotta cheese
- 1 tablespoon chopped fresh coriander (cilantro)
- 1 tablespoon chopped fresh basil
- 1 tablespoon chopped fresh chives
- 1 garlic clove, put through a garlic press
  Freshly ground white pepper to taste
  Vegetable seasoning to taste

Wash and dry the celery stalks.

In a small bowl, mix together all the remaining ingredients. Spread the filling in the stalks with a small spatula, or pipe it from a pastry bag fitted with a star tip. Arrange on a serving dish with the stuffed cherry tomatoes.

### SERVES 8

# SWISS CHARD AND GRUYÈRE SPREAD

## 116
### CALORIES PER SERVING

This subtlely spiced spread may be prepared the night before the party and stored, tightly covered, in the refrigerator. The subtle blend of flavors can be most appreciated when the spread is served at room temperature. Use a low-calorie cracker like Swedish flat breads, only 20 calories apiece.

16 Swiss chard stalks
1 tablespoon extra-virgin olive oil
1 small white onion, finely chopped
1 small garlic clove, minced
6 ounces Gruyère cheese, grated
Freshly ground white pepper to taste
Vegetable seasoning to taste

### GARNISH
4 cherry tomatoes, halved

Remove the heavy stems from the chard and discard. Wash the leaves, pat dry, and chop coarsely.

Heat the olive oil in a skillet, add the onion, and sauté over medium heat for 3 minutes. Add the garlic and chard and sauté for 4 to 5 minutes more, stirring often. Add the cheese and toss in the skillet for 1 minute, then add the seasonings. Turn the mixture into a food processor and purée. Transfer to a bowl and let cool. The spread can be chilled if made ahead of time, and allowed to return to room temperature.

Spread on crackers and decorate with cherry tomato halves.

### SERVES 8

# SCALLOP SEVICHE ON CUCUMBER ROUNDS

## 61
### CALORIES PER SERVING

Delicate sea scallops are gently "cooked" overnight in their citrus acid bath of lemon and lime juices and served on cool cucumber rounds—a pungent hors d'oeuvre. Chilled seviche also makes a tasty (and easy) appetizer for a hot summer menu. If you prefer, substitute very fresh sea bass for the scallops.

Freshly squeezed juice of 3 limes
Freshly squeezed juice of 1 lemon
2 tablespoons extra-virgin olive oil
8 large sea scallops (about 8 ounces), each cut crosswise into 2 disks
1/4 cup minced onion
1 tomato, peeled, seeded, and cut into 1/4-inch dice
1 tablespoon chopped fresh coriander
16 (1/4-inch) slices cucumber, peeled only if cucumbers are waxed

### GARNISH
1/4 red pepper, cut into thin julienne strips

Mix the lime juice, lemon juice, and olive oil in a bowl. Add the scallops and toss to mix well. Cover with plastic wrap and leave in the refrigerator overnight. Stir once or twice.

Just before serving, drain the scallops and toss with the onion, tomato, and coriander. Place a scallop slice on each cucumber round, arrange on a serving plate, decorate with red pepper strips, and serve.

### SERVES 8

# SALMON AND TUNA SASHIMI

## 56
### CALORIES PER SERVING

Use only the freshest fish for sashimi. If tuna is out of season, substitute bass, sea or bay scallops, or whatever fish your eye and nose tell you is super-fresh. Buy the fish on the day you serve it, keep it refrigerated, and do not slice until just before serving.

2 tablespoons dry Japanese horseradish (wasabi)
1/4 pound lightly smoked or cured salmon
1/4 pound fresh tuna
1/4 cup low-sodium soy sauce

Prepare the horseradish by adding enough water to make a firm paste. Shape the paste into a cone and place in a small dish.

Cut the fish across the grain into thin slices and arrange on a chilled plate. Pour the soy sauce into a small bowl. Arrange the horseradish, fish, and soy sauce on a tray and serve. (It might be wise to tell your guests that the horseradish is very strong and should be used with caution.)

### SERVES 8

# FALL HOLIDAY DINNER

CRISP APPLE AND
WALNUT SALAD
WITH HONEY-YOGURT
DRESSING

REVOLUTIONARY
ROAST TURKEY

CRANBERRY-MUSHROOM
STUFFING

GIBLET GRAVY

ACORN SQUASH PURÉE

ROSEBUD
BRUSSELS SPROUTS

PUMPKIN MOUSSE

HERBAL TEA OR
DECAFFEINATED COFFEE

WINE SUGGESTION:
SAUVIGNON BLANC

# CRISP APPLE AND WALNUT SALAD WITH HONEY-YOGURT DRESSING

## 134
CALORIES PER SERVING

This refreshing salad combines crisp apples, crunchy celery, and chopped walnuts in a creamy lemon-honey yogurt sauce. It's especially good in the fall, made with the firmest apples. Whether making this for family or friends, you'll want to mix up the dressing ahead and prepare the apples as close to serving time as possible, to preserve their crispness and keep them from turning brown. Freshly shelled walnuts are best.

### HONEY-YOGURT DRESSING
- ½ cup soft tofu
- ½ cup plain low-fat yogurt
  Juice of ½ lemon
- 3 tablespoons honey
  Pinch of barley malt sweetener

- ¼ cup fresh lemon juice
- 5 McIntosh or other crisp apples
- 3 celery stalks, cut into ½-inch dice
- ⅓ cup coarsely chopped walnuts
- 8 leaves butter (Boston) lettuce

### GARNISH
- 8 sprigs fresh mint

**TO PREPARE THE DRESSING:** Combine all the ingredients in a blender and purée. Pour into a bowl, cover with plastic wrap, and refrigerate until serving time.

**TO PREPARE THE APPLES:** Combine the lemon juice and 1 cup of water in a large bowl. Cut the apples into eighths, remove the core and seeds, and immediately place in the acidulated water. When all the apples have been put into the bowl, add additional water to cover.

At serving time, drain the apples, discarding the lemon water. Combine the apples, celery, walnuts, and dressing and toss gently.

Place a lettuce leaf on each of 8 salad plates, spoon salad into the leaves, top with mint, and serve.

**SERVES 8**

# REVOLUTIONARY ROAST TURKEY

## 253
CALORIES PER SERVING

Our relatively rapid method for roasting turkey will revolutionize your attitude toward the bird's possibilities, and you will start serving it more often. Most recipes for roast turkey call for trussing the bird and roasting it until the thigh joint moves easily in the socket, 3 to 3½ hours for a 6- to 8-pound turkey. The problem with this method is that the trussed legs and thighs are pressed up tight against the body and don't get enough heat. By the time they are cooked, the breast meat is dried out and tasteless.

In this recipe, the turkey is not trussed. Instead, an incision is made into the leg at the knee joint, and the legs and thighs are left to dangle open, exposed to sufficient heat to cook them at the same rate as the breast.

This way, the turkey roasts for only 1½ hours and the breast meat is juicy and flavorful.

Fresh organically raised turkey is preferable for reasons of both flavor and nutrition, but a good-quality frozen one will do very well. We do not recommend buying self-basting turkeys, however; the chemical additives involved in this process rob the turkey of its taste.

1 (6- to 8-pound) turkey
Freshly ground white pepper to taste
Vegetable seasoning to taste
1 tablespoon cold-pressed oil

Preheat the oven to 350°F.
Wash the turkey inside and out with cold water, taking care to remove any extraneous fat and blood from the cavity. Pat the bird dry. Rub the cavity with pepper and vegetable seasoning, then spoon in the stuffing. Place a small square of foil over the exposed stuffing and smooth the edges of the foil inside the cavity to hold the stuffing in place.

Place the turkey on its back with the legs pointing toward you. With the point of a sharp knife, make an incision on the inside of one leg where the thigh meets the drumstick. Cut toward the joint, jiggling the knife until it hits the bone; do not cut through the tendon. Make an incision in the other leg.

Rub the turkey skin all over with oil, place the bird on a rack in a roasting pan, and roast for about 1½ hours, or until the thigh juices run clear. Because it cooks so quickly, the turkey will not need basting.

Remove the turkey from the oven and transfer to a carving board. Before carving, allow the bird to rest for 10 to 15 minutes while you make the gravy.

When you are ready to serve, remove the pieces of foil covering the cavity and spoon the stuffing into a serving bowl. Then carve the turkey and serve.

SERVES 8

# CRANBERRY-MUSHROOM STUFFING

## 200
### CALORIES PER SERVING

This nutty stuffing will get rave reviews, especially if you can find fresh sage, which is often available in the fall. The cranberries, soaked in sweetened water long enough to blunt their tartness, cook while they're in the turkey. Wild mushrooms, which are plentiful at this time of year, will add another dimension to the stuffing's flavor.

1 teaspoon barley malt sweetener
2 cups water
2 tablespoons honey
1½ cups fresh cranberries or thawed frozen cranberries
½ loaf Cinnamon-Orange Poppy Seed Bread (page 38)
1 tablespoon unsalted butter
1 large onion, coarsely chopped
1½ tablespoons chopped fresh sage or 1 teaspoon dried
1 celery stalk, cut into ¼-inch dice
2 pounds small mushrooms, quartered
1 egg, beaten
½ cup nonfat skim milk
½ cup coarsely chopped pecans

In a mixing bowl, combine the barley malt sweetener, water, and honey. Stir in the cranberries and let stand for 2 hours.

To make croutons, preheat the oven to 200°F. Trim the crust off the bread and cut the bread into ½-inch cubes. Spread the cubes in one layer on a baking sheet and bake for 3 to 5 minutes. The croutons will become drier as they cool. Set aside.

Melt the butter in a large skillet, add the onion, and sauté over medium heat for 3 to 5 minutes. Add the sage and celery and toss to combine. Remove from the heat, add the mushrooms, and toss again. Set aside to cool.

Mix together the egg and milk. Strain the cranberries and discard the liquid.

In a large mixing bowl, toss the croutons with the onion-mushroom mixture. Add the cranberries and pecans and toss again. Add the egg mixture and toss for 30 seconds. The stuffing is now ready to use.

SERVES 8

RECIPES CONTINUE ON PAGE 150.

# GIBLET GRAVY

## 26
CALORIES PER SERVING

To avoid last-minute crises, you can make the turkey stock the night before the party and finish the gravy after the turkey has roasted. Allow 2 tablespoons for each serving.

   Neck and wing tips from turkey
1  quart Chicken Stock (page 161)
1  onion, quartered
2  carrots, peeled and cut into 1-inch pieces
1  celery stalk, cut into 1-inch pieces
1  sprig Italian parsley
   Turkey giblets and heart
   Freshly ground white pepper to taste
   Vegetable seasoning to taste

Preheat the oven to 350°F.
   Spread the neck and wing tips on a baking sheet and brown in the oven for 25 to 30 minutes. Transfer them to a large pot, add the stock, onion, carrots, celery, and parsley, and bring to a boil. Lower the heat, cover the pot, and simmer slowly for 3 to 4 hours, skimming as needed. Strain the stock, discarding the solids. Cool the broth, then refrigerate.
   Trim the thick membrane from the giblets. Cut the giblets and heart into ¼-inch dice. Blanch for 1 minute in a cup of boiling water, drain, and reserve.

After the turkey is roasted, pour off the grease and deglaze the pan with 2 cups of the turkey stock, scraping up the brown bits. Pour into a pot, add the remaining stock and the giblets, and bring to a boil. Boil rapidly, uncovered, for 5 to 8 minutes, reducing by half. Add pepper and vegetable seasoning. The sauce should have a syruplike consistency.
   Pour into a heated gravy boat and serve.

**SERVES 8**

# ACORN SQUASH PURÉE

## 65
CALORIES PER SERVING

A traditional accompaniment to turkey, the squash may be prepared early in the day and put in the oven 10 minutes after the turkey comes out.

4  medium acorn squash
½  cup soft tofu
1  egg plus 2 egg whites
⅛  teaspoon ground allspice
2  tablespoons honey
   Freshly ground white pepper to taste
1  tablespoon melted butter
   Cinnamon, allspice, and/or freshly ground nutmeg to taste

Preheat the oven to 350°F.
   Cut the squash in half lengthwise, scrape out the seeds, place cut side down on a baking sheet, and bake until soft, about 1 hour.
   When cool enough to handle, scoop out the flesh into a mixing bowl and mash well. Add the tofu and blend thoroughly. In another bowl, beat the egg and egg whites lightly, then add the squash mixture, spices, honey, pepper, and butter. Mix well.
   Turn the purée into a shallow 1-quart baking dish. If preparing ahead to this point, cover the dish with wax paper.
   Preheat the oven to 350°F. Bake for 30 minutes. Serve hot, sprinkled with additional allspice, cinnamon, or nutmeg (or all three), if desired.

**SERVES 8**

# ROSEBUD BRUSSELS SPROUTS

## 23
CALORIES PER SERVING

Belgium's best ambassadors, these rosebud cabbages are a fall crop, so they will be fresh for your holiday dinner. Buy the smallest and tightest buds you can find. Smaller sprouts are more delicate in flavor and texture than the larger ones. Garden-fresh sprouts are crisp to the fingernail and bright green to the eye. These marvelous mini-cabbages are rich in vitamin A and potassium.

2 pints Brussels sprouts
1 tablespoon unsalted butter
  Freshly ground white pepper to taste
  Vegetable seasoning to taste

Prepare the sprouts by removing any wilted or damaged leaves. Rinse well. with a sharp knife, cut an X ¼ inch deep in the root end of each sprout, to allow the water to penetrate to the center of the vegetable and cook it more evenly.

Bring 2 quarts of water to a boil, add the sprouts, return to a boil, and cook, uncovered, for 6 to 8 minutes, or until the vegetables are crisp-tender. Do not overcook; mushy sprouts lose all their flavor. While the sprouts are boiling, fill a large bowl with cold water. Drain the sprouts and refresh in the water. When they have cooled, drain and pat dry.

Just before serving, melt the butter in a skillet over medium heat. Add the sprouts, and toss with the butter until hot. Season with pepper and vegetable seasoning, and serve.

SERVES 8

# PUMPKIN MOUSSE

## 154
CALORIES PER SERVING

We bake these little desserts in flowerpot-shaped dariole molds, but they will taste just as good made in individual soufflé molds or a larger soufflé dish.

2 eggs, lightly beaten
¼ cup honey
2 teaspoons date sugar
1 teaspoon ground cinnamon
  Pinch of ground cloves
  Pinch of ground mace
⅛ teaspoon freshly grated nutmeg
1 tablespoon dry skim milk
1 (14-ounce) can unsweetened pumpkin purée
1 cup half-and-half
1 recipe Spa Cream (page 27), made without sweetener

Preheat the oven to 325°F. for smaller molds or 300°F. for one large dish. Butter eight ½-cup soufflé molds or a 1-quart soufflé dish.

Whisk the eggs in a mixing bowl, add the honey, Equal, spices, and dry milk, and mix well. Add the pumpkin and half-and-half and whisk until completely blended. Pour into the molds. Place the molds in a baking pan at least 1½ or 2 inches deep. Pour enough very hot tap water into the baking pan to reach halfway up the molds.

Bake the smaller molds for 40 to 50 minutes, the 1-quart dish for 1¼ hours. Remove the molds from the baking pan and let cool to room temperature.

To serve, run a knife around the edges of the molds and invert the mousses onto 8 dessert plates.

Make the Spa Cream and decorate the mousses with tiny rosettes piped from a pastry bag fitted with a small star tip. Or, simply place a dollop of the cream on top of each mousse. Serve at once.

SERVES 8

SPA
BASICS

The secret to success is constancy to purpose.

—BENJAMIN DISRAELI

It's never easy to make major changes in your life-style, much less to stick with them, but over the years we've learned there are things you can do to make the transition less painful. Here are some of the "secrets" that we've shared with our guests.

E at regular meals and time them to coincide with periods of activity during your day. The identical meal eaten at different times will be burned by the body at different rates. For instance, body metabolism is slowest when you're asleep, faster after exercise and other physical exertion, so try to eat dinner at least three hours before retiring. Don't skip meals. Going without breakfast or lunch will only make you insatiable at dinner, and eating three regular meals, ideally at the same time each day, also helps maintain even blood sugar and constant energy levels.

Drink lots of mineral water throughout the day—at least six 8-ounce glasses. Not only is this marvelous for the complexion, but it will keep you feeling full and satisfy your need for oral gratification. Try mixing a little fruit juice with mineral water to be taken a half hour before meals; because it takes your body 20 minutes to register that you have eaten, the juice "cocktail" will cut your appetite by raising your blood sugar level.

If you are feeling particularly ravenous, fill up on fiber, large salads, and low-calorie vegetables (see "free foods," page 63). Just be aware that while salads are low-calorie, the oils in dressings are not; to save calories, you can dilute salad dressing with water and spray it on with a plant sprayer. In this way, you avoid saturating the lettuce.

Where you eat can also affect your appetite. Eat only in a proper dining setting. Do not, for instance, nibble in front of the television, in front of the refrigerator, in bed, or in the bathtub except on special occasions. If you do, you risk developing a conditioned reflex.

W hen dining out, you will need to adapt the regimen to your life-style. Like Odysseus steering a safe passage between Scylla and Charybdis, you must anticipate potential dangers and devise a strategy to navigate successfully toward controlled calorie intake.

In restaurants, it is really quite easy to cut calories if you make your selections with care. For cocktails, opt for mineral waters or club soda, with a slice of lemon, lime, or orange for color and flavor; or try a light wine spritzer. If your compatriots agree, ask that bread and butter be cleared off the table immediately to avoid impatient nibbling.

In general, stay away from foods prepared with butter and oil (sautéed or fried) and those that come in cream sauce. Instead, order dishes that are grilled, broiled, poached, steamed, or roasted. For appetizers, quiches and pâtés are out, as is anything in butter (escargots), cream (coquilles St. Jacques), or mayonnaise (mussels ravigote). Substitute sea-food cocktails with lemon, salads of all kinds, vegetables, fruit, fresh juices, and clear soups.

For a main course, choose fish, chicken, and veal over beef, pork, and lamb. Eat poultry without the skin, except, of course, in the case of birds like quail, where this would be impossible. Train your eye to portion control; learn to recognize a 4-ounce portion of fish, chicken, or veal, and simply stop eating there. Don't feel shy about requesting smaller portions. Guests at our café, Jack's, do it all the time and nobody's feelings get hurt. Request that all sauces, gravies, and salad dressings be served on the side, and use them sparingly: take one or two tablespoons at most, then have the waiter take them away.

If you are still hungry after the main course, order a salad in lieu of dessert. If you must have a sweet finish, fresh berries or ripe fruits are best. If you decide to splurge on a fattening dessert, do it with a friend (or friends) and share the calories. Another suggestion that requires a little more willpower (but we've seen it done): order the dessert you want and take just one bite.

Business lunches and social drinking can be difficult because of peer pressure and for other reasons. However, in a business situation especially, if you demonstrate that you are in control of yourself and of what you eat, that quality of command will gain you respect. If you must order a bottle of wine, limit yourself to one glass. Be direct about your motivation. People admire openness and honesty.

Cocktail parties and social drinking are other times to test your control over temptation. The best diet tactic is to say "No, thank you" to hard liquor and rich hors d'oeuvres. Never feel you must apologize. Stick to a mineral water, munch the crudités, and concentrate on enjoying the company instead.

Even if you are not able to fit a full-fledged workout into your schedule on a given day (and exercise *should* be a part of your daily agenda every day), you can still sneak in a couple minutes of well-spent exercise time. If you are stranded in the office, don't make excuses—leg lifts can be done sitting down, and pressing palms together for pectoral muscles requires no special equipment. Or concentrate on improving your posture, keeping your stomach tight, your shoulders down and back, your spine long and straight, chin high. Walk everywhere that you possibly can rather than driving, and if you must take public transportation for a short distance, stand rather than sit. Although these mini-exercises won't take the place of your regular routine of aerobic exercise, they will help put a little spring in your step, reduce fatigue and tension, and motivate you to give a bit more when you do find the time to work out.

By adhering to these simple commonsense guidelines, you should be able to make the Spa life-style your life-style, without compromising your social life. We are not advocating abstinence, just moderation and self-control. Be good to yourself. Enjoy life and make it a long, healthy one.

# EXERCISE: A WAY OF LIFE

The secret ingredient in any recipe for health and beauty is a regular program of exercise, and the Spa program is no exception. The success and spectacular results we obtain here are due entirely to the critical combination of diet *and* exercise. And just as the Spa's dietary regimen can be followed at home, for maximum, lasting health benefits you also need to incorporate exercise into your life-style.

This does not mean a return to Puritanism. Ours is really a very modest proposal: a program of exercise combining a 30-minute aerobic activity three or four times weekly with a brisk 30-minute walk daily. (Brisk, by the way, is not window-shopping speed.) Plan exercise as part of your weekly schedule so it becomes a habit. This, however, is a *minimal* workout, which will help keep you toned and cardiovascularly fit but will not increase your weight loss. To burn more calories and fat, you must increase your activity level beyond these guidelines. Dieting is not enough.

There is a reason that diet alone does not work. When you cut calories, the body's metabolism slows down to protect its fat stores. So when you resume normal eating, your sluggish metabolism can even make you gain by failing to burn calories at your usual rate. However, the proper kind of exercise can effectively speed up a miserly metabolism, using up calories *faster*.

By proper exercise we mean steady, low-intensity aerobics, such as jogging, swimming, rowing, or bicycling. In fact, any continuous whole-body movement, even brisk walking, burns 50 to 100 percent more calories than any calisthentic-type workout. (Contrary to popular belief, fat is not reduced by spot conditioning.)

Aerobic exercise on a regular basis has numerous physical and psychological benefits. But it also makes a dramatic difference in any weight-loss program. Cutting calories without aerobic exercise will cause you to lose half the weight in fat and half in muscle protein, a result even the most devout dieter would wish to avoid. With aerobic activity you will lose 100 percent fat, providing you do not exceed your maximum training heart rate (220 minus your age). A bonus for the lazy person in all of us is the fact that aerobic activity stimulates the production of myoglobin, mitochondria, and fat-burning enzymes, enhancing fat loss for several hours after exercising—even during rest.

*When* you exercise is also important because you tend to burn more calories in a given activity when body metabolism is at a high point. The naturally occurring highs each day are late in the afternoon, from 4:00 P.M. to 8:00 P.M., and after meals. So to maximize the profits of your investment, work out in the late afternoon (which has the added advantage of cutting your appetite for dinner), and take a brisk walk after meals.

Proper breathing is also critical. If you find yourself breathless, you are working too hard: only low-intensity aerobic exercise burns fat, so your pulse should be kept at 60 percent of your theoretical maximum. Another good rule of thumb is that you should be able to carry on a conversation as you exercise. You do not want to work so hard that you end up panting: this causes you to burn mostly glucose and makes you hungrier!

After strenuous exercise, allow a period for "cooling down." Blood pressure must gradually drop back to normal, and the blood that has gone to your limbs during your workout needs time to return to the heart—otherwise a blackout could occur. Continue to move slowly and concentrate on muscles you have just worked—for example, the hamstring and calf muscles after running. Inhale deeply. Stretching helps give your body the long smooth lines of a gymnast, as opposed to the short bulky muscles of a weight lifter.

To begin your exercise program, do not wait for inspiration to strike. Start with a plan. First, find an aerobic activity you enjoy because, quite simply, if you don't take pleasure in it, chances are you will not do it very long. Make it convenient to your home or office. Do some preliminary research by asking your fitness-minded friends which gyms and instructors are best. Experiment with different classes in your neighborhood. There are many styles of teaching aerobics and different kinds of music; even the same method taught by a different teacher can make all the difference. You may find you prefer jazz to country, the Beatles to Beethoven, or an ecumenical variety.

Classes have several advantages. There are no telephone interruptions, no refrigerators, and no lack of space or equipment. Being with a group of people all interested in fitness gives you positive energy and motivation, while a teacher encourages you to get the most out of an exercise and checks that you are always in the correct position, reducing the possibility of injury or strain. And the supportive atmosphere of working with others toward a mutual goal makes exercising a more pleasant, rewarding activity. Finally, setting aside a regular time for exercising is far more reliable than the whims of willpower.

If you choose to exercise on your own, which, of course, has the advantage of flexibility in terms of time, you should still have a goal-oriented plan and set schedule. This could be jogging or swimming three times a week, either mornings before work, evenings after work, or as an energizing lunch break. You may begin by running half a mile and plan to increase it a little each week until you work up to three or four; you may start off swimming 20 laps and work up to 40 or 50. Don't push yourself too hard or be overly ambitious. Before embarking on any strenuous exercise program, consult with your medical doctor or a professional fitness instructor.

Using machines at home for aerobic conditioning is another option. Stationary bicycles, treadmills, and rebound trampolines for running are readily available. Even better is a rowing machine, which strengthens arms, legs, and back muscles. The best workout for cardiovascular fitness and overall body conditioning is a cross-country skiing machine.

At home you can also do a variety of spot conditioning routines to limber, strengthen, and tone muscles. We recommend pushups for arms, chest, and upper back; half sit-ups for abdominals and waist; and leg lifts for hips and thighs. To build up specific muscle groups, lifting free weights is excellent but should be supervised initially, since it can cause back strain.

Yes, there can be boredom in exercise, so try to find an activity you enjoy. There are also ways to distract yourself: play music that you like, watch television, exercise with your spouse or a friend. Just resolve that exercising daily is just as important as brushing your teeth in the morning—if not more so!

The benefits of regular aerobic exercise are not only a better body but also a more radiant complexion, improved skin tone and elasticity, and healthier hair and nails. It improves circulation, reduces cholesterol, strengthens heart muscles, lowers blood pressure and pulse rate, cuts appetite, regulates blood sugar levels, and helps you sleep better.

There are also more subtle benefits, such as reducing stress. Stress is as harmful to your health as poor nutrition, and although you certainly cannot avoid it in modern life, you can learn to deal with it successfully, minimizing its ill effects. One way to reduce stress is to recognize it when it occurs: be aware when your neck muscles tense, your stomach gets butterflies, or you feel anxious or jittery. Everyone's stress symptoms are different. Learn where your stress points are; then consciously focus on relaxing these parts of your body. Inhaling deeply, sending oxygen to the tensed areas helps; so does stretching, closing your eyes for a few moments, and, of course, exercising.

In our stress-management class, we teach a combination of yoga stretches, followed by progressive relaxation, beginning with your big toe and ending with your facial muscles. Learning to relax facial muscles could save you years of worry lines! Dealing with stress is simply another dimension of self-awareness: it is really about getting in touch with and controlling your body, making it work for you.

Your body is an amazing machine. One of our spa directors makes this perceptive analogy: "If you could own only one car in your lifetime, a very finely tuned piece of equipment such as a Ferrari or a Rolls-Royce, you would certainly take good care of it. You would not let the engine get dirty or run down, you wouldn't forget to change the oil regularly or to feed it with the proper fuel. Well, your body is a fantastic mechanism, and it needs good care. It likes to be taken out on the road; it likes to run. It must have regular checkups. And it always needs good fuel."

Regular exercise, fresh, wholesome food, and ample time for relaxation—these are the ingredients that make up the recipe for a healthier, more vital life. As the body gets older, its requirements change. Learn to pay attention to your body and the signals it sends, and respond to those signals; it's the only body you have; it's a precious gift; be good to it.

Quality stocks are fundamentals of every cuisine. Used as the base for soups and sauces and as a poaching medium, flavorful homemade stock is also indispensable to Spa cuisine. Although cooking time may be somewhat lengthy, nothing could be simpler than making stock—and, for the rich results, well worth the time and effort. Here are a few points to consider before you begin.

### INGREDIENTS

Stock is only as good as the ingredients that go into it, so use only the best vegetables available. Wrinkled carrots, dried-out garlic, and limp celery do not belong in stock; their flavor and nutritional value is long gone. On the other hand, save and freeze chicken and veal bones and trimmings and chopped-up shrimp and lobster shells, ingredients that will enrich the broth.

### SKIMMING

As they first come to a boil, chicken and veal bones release a good deal of scum, which, left in the pot, will turn the stock cloudy and bitter. Skim often during this initial period, using a large spoon or wire skimmer. After the stock is at a simmer, it will need skimming only occasionally. Fish stock needs no skimming.

### COOKING TIME

The cooking times, which are different for each stock, are based on the length of time it takes to extract the flavor from each combination of bones and vegetables with the liquid at a simmer. Once the stock is simmering, it is unwise to return it to a

boil. For one thing, you run the risk of burning the bones and vegetables at the bottom of the pot. Additionally, unskimmed fat and debris may be sucked back into the stock, with the adverse effects already mentioned. Finally, boiling liquid evaporates too quickly to extract all the flavor from the bones and you will have to add more water, which will dilute the stock. You can, however, stop cooking the stock at any point after it has simmered for 30 minutes. To finish cooking, return to a boil, lower the heat, and simmer for the amount of time indicated in the recipe.

### COOLING THE STOCK

After cooking and straining, let the stock cool at room temperature, uncovered. Chill overnight in the refrigerator and then remove the fat that has congealed on the surface. If you will be using the stock within a day or two, store in the refrigerator; otherwise, freeze it. It will keep for 4 to 6 months.

## FISH STOCK

### 12
#### CALORIES PER QUART

Fish Stock is very easy to make; it cooks for only 30 minutes and need not be watched once it is at a simmer. As the poaching medium for halibut and salmon (pages 50 and 55) or for boiling lobsters (page 70), Fish Stock is incomparably superior to water, because it enhances the flavor of the fish instead of leaching it away. Once it is made, the stock can be used and re-used several times. In some of our recipes we suggest that you strain any stock left after poaching and freeze it to use in other recipes. Each time the stock is recycled, its flavor is enriched, and after two or three cycles you will have a splendid fish soup to use as the base for a potatoless chowder. When you buy the fish bones, ask your fishmonger to give you only the heads and bones of white-fleshed, nonoily fish (sole, flounder, whitefish, bass, halibut, etc.), gills removed.

 5 pounds fish bones (gills removed) from white-fleshed fish
 1 gallon water
 1 onion, cut into wedges
 1 celery stalk, sliced
 1 sprig Italian parsley
 ¼ cup chopped mushrooms or mushroom trimmings
 1 tablespoon white peppercorns
 1 cup dry white wine (optional)

Wash the fish bones under cold running water and remove any blood or entrails. Put in a large soup kettle with all the remaining ingredients and bring to a boil over high heat. Reduce the heat and simmer, uncovered, for 30 minutes. (Further cooking would make the stock bitter.) Strain through a fine sieve and discard the bones and vegetables. Unless the stock is to be used immediately let cool, uncovered, to room temperature.

**MAKES 3 QUARTS**

## CHICKEN STOCK

### 18
CALORIES PER QUART

Because the light flavor of Chicken Stock combines well with almost any vegetable, we use it as the base for many of our Spa soups. For the bones, you can either buy backs, necks, and wing tips, or you can save and freeze raw chicken trimmings and the bones from roast chicken. Do not use the liver or giblets, because they impart a bitter taste to the stock.

5 pounds chicken bones
1 gallon water
1 large carrot, peeled and cut into chunks
1 celery stalk
1 large onion, cut into chunks
1 tablespoon white peppercorns
1 bay leaf
1 sprig Italian parsley

Wash the chicken bones in cold water and put them in an 8-quart stockpot with all the remaining ingredients. Set the pot over high heat and bring to a boil, removing the scum and fat as they rise to the surface with a spoon or a wire skimmer. Lower the heat so that the liquid barely simmers. Do *not* let it return to a boil. Cook, uncovered, for 4 hours, continuing to skim as necessary.

Strain the stock, discarding the bones and vegetables, and let cool, uncovered, at room temperature. Refrigerate and skim off any fat remaining in the stock, which will congeal on top.

**MAKES 2 QUARTS**

## RICH CHICKEN STOCK

### 12
CALORIES PER CUP

Chicken Stock is enriched by the addition of more bones and fresh vegetables and then reduced to concentrate the flavor. This is, in effect, a double reduction. Serve the stock by itself as old-fashioned chicken soup, or use it as a flavorful base for other soups.

1 pound chicken bones and trimmings
½ large carrot, peeled and cut into chunks
½ stalk celery, cut into chunks
½ large onion, cut into wedges
1½ teaspoons white peppercorns
½ bay leaf
1 sprig Italian parsley
2 quarts cold Chicken Stock (preceding recipe) or salt-free canned chicken broth

Bring all the ingredients to a boil, reduce the heat, and simmer the broth, uncovered, for 1 hour, skimming it often. Strain, let cool, chill, and remove the congealed fat from the surface.

**MAKES 1½ QUARTS**

# SHALLOT-SCENTED CHICKEN SAUCE

## 31

CALORIES PER ¼ CUP

A further reduction, this time of Rich Chicken Stock, once again using fresh chicken bones, shallots, and mush-rooms. The stock is lightly thickened with arrowroot and wine, and the re-sult is a sauce with an intense chicken flavor and very few calories. Serve the sauce with roast or broiled chicken, rice, or bulgur.

- 1 pound chicken bones and trimmings
- 3 shallots, peeled and chopped
- ¼ cup chopped mushrooms or mushroom trimmings
- 1½ quarts cold Rich Chicken Stock (preceding recipe)
- 2 tablespoons arrowroot mixed with 2 tablespoons dry white wine

Put the bones, shallots, mush-rooms, and stock in a 3-quart pot and bring to a boil over high heat, skim-ming constantly. Lower the heat and simmer, uncovered, until reduced by half, skimming often. Return to a boil and whisk in the arrowroot mixture, which will instantly thicken the sauce. Reduce the heat and simmer for 5 minutes more. Strain, let cool, chill, and remove the congealed fat.

MAKES ABOUT 3 CUPS

# VEAL STOCK

## 56

CALORIES PER QUART

This stock is a good foundation for soups, especially onion soup. It is also the base for a double reduction or doubly rich stock and a wonderful veal sauce. For Veal Stock the bones and vegetables are first browned in the oven to give the stock color. Rib ends from breast of veal or meaty knuckle bones make delicious stock. Ask your butcher to cut the bones into 2-inch pieces. This will make them easier to fit into the pot and will provide more surfaces to brown, thus deepening the color and flavor of the stock.

- 5 pounds veal bones, cut into 2-inch pieces
- 1 large carrot, peeled and cut into chunks
- 1 large onion, chopped
- 1½ gallons water
- 1 celery stalk, cut into chunks
- 2 garlic cloves
- 1 tablespoon white peppercorns
- 2 bay leaves
- 1 tablespoon fresh thyme or 1½ teaspoons dried
- 3 tablespoons tomato purée
- 1 cup white wine

Preheat the oven to 350°F.
Spread the veal bones in a large shallow baking pan and bake for 10 minutes. Add the carrot and onion and continue to bake for 10 minutes, or until the bones, carrot, and onion are golden brown. (Do not brown the celery, which would make it bitter.)

Put the bones and vegetables in an 8-quart stockpot and add all the remaining ingredients. Pour 1 cup of water into the roasting pan and, with a wooden spoon, stir up all the browned bits of meat and vegetable, then pour the deglazing liquid into the stockpot. Bring the stock to a boil over high heat, skimming often as scum and fat rise to the surface (veal releases a lot of scum). Reduce the heat so that the liquid barely simmers, and cook, uncovered, for 6 hours, skimming as necessary.

Strain into a bowl and let cool, uncovered, at room temperature. Chill the stock, then remove any fat that has congealed at the top.

MAKES 2 QUARTS

# RICH VEAL STOCK

## 36

CALORIES PER CUP

Use this double reduction as a soup base when you want a richer, more intense meat flavor.

- 1 tablespoon cold-pressed vegetable oil
- 1 pound veal or chicken bones and trimmings, cut into 2-inch pieces
- ½ large onion, chopped
- ½ large carrot, peeled and sliced
- 1½ teaspoons white peppercorns
- ½ bay leaf
- 1 sprig Italian parsley
- 2 quarts cold Veal Stock (preceding recipe)

Heat the oil in a 4-quart pot, add the veal bones, onion, and carrot, and sauté over high heat for 4 minutes, stirring constantly to prevent burning. Add all the remaining ingredients, bring to a boil, and lower the heat. Simmer the broth, uncovered, for 1 hour and skim it as necessary. Strain, let cool, chill, and remove the congealed fat.

**MAKES 1½ QUARTS**

# VEAL MUSHROOM SAUCE

## 56

CALORIES PER ¼ CUP

This triply reduced veal stock makes a marvelous sauce served by itself with grilled or roast veal or, even better, enhanced with sliced wild or button mushrooms lightly sautéed in a little butter. It is also a flavorful braising liquid for fennel, endive, and celery.

- 1 tablespoon cold-pressed vegetable oil
- 1 pound veal or chicken bones and trimmings, cut into 2-inch pieces
- 3 shallots, peeled and minced
- ¼ cup chopped mushrooms or mushroom trimmings
- 1½ quarts cold Rich Veal Stock (preceding recipe)
- 2 tablespoons arrowroot mixed with 2 tablespoons white wine

In a 3-quart pot, heat the oil, add the veal bones, and brown over high heat for 3 to 5 minutes, stirring constantly. Add the shallots and mushrooms and toss for 1 minute, taking care that the shallots do not burn. Add the stock and bring to a boil over high heat, skimming off the scum and fat that rise to the surface. Lower the heat and simmer, uncovered, until reduced by half, skimming often. When the stock is reduced, return it to a boil and whisk in the arrowroot mixture, which will instantly thicken the sauce. Reduce the heat, simmer for 5 minutes, then strain, let cool, and refrigerate. Remove any congealed fat.

**MAKES 3 CUPS**

# VEGETABLE BROTH

## 84

CALORIES PER QUART

This vitamin-rich broth can be used as a base for a hearty vegetable soup, to add savor to a vegetable as it is braised, or as a good substitute for Chicken Stock in soup recipes. In addition to the vegetables listed in the ingredients, asparagus stems and mushroom trimmings may be put into the stock. Do not use cabbage, broccoli, kale, or Brussels sprouts, unless you want a very strong flavor. Other herbs, such as basil, tarragon, or dill, will also enhance the broth. All the vegetables and herbs should be in peak condition; damaged, wilted, or wrinkled vegetables have lost most of their nutritional value and flavor.

- 1 gallon water
- 2 onions, cut into wedges
- 4 celery stalks, thickly sliced
- 3 carrots, peeled and thickly sliced
- 2 leeks (white part only), washed and thickly sliced
- 2 turnips, peeled and cut into wedges
- 1 zucchini, ends trimmed, thickly sliced
- 1 red or green pepper, stemmed, seeded, and cut into chunks
- 4 tomatoes, seeded and coarsely chopped
- 3 garlic cloves
- 2 sprigs Italian parsley
- 2 bay leaves
- 1 tablespoon fresh thyme or 1½ teaspoons dried
- 10 black peppercorns

Put all ingredients in a large stockpot. Bring to a boil, then lower the heat and simmer, uncovered, very slowly for 2 hours. Strain the stock, discarding the solids. Let cool to room temperature.

**MAKES 2 QUARTS**

## THINGS TO BUY FRESH

### FRUITS AND VEGETABLES

Fruits and vegetables taste incomparably better and are at their most nutritious eaten in season. The lucky few who grow their own, or who cultivate friends who cultivate gardens, will know the intense pleasure of plucking a vine-ripened tomato and eating it at once, still warm from the sun. For the rest of us, a reliable greengrocer is the answer. Try to shop for fruits and vegetables every day, and use the produce immediately. Flabby zucchini tastes flabby. However, some fruits—tomatoes, papayas, mangoes—can be brought to a fuller ripeness if left in a sunny window for a day or two.

Experiment with unfamiliar vegetables if your favorites are out of season. Kale, for instance, is an often-overlooked winter vegetable that is rich in iron and calcium, and parsnips and turnips deserve attention too. Or try acorn or spaghetti squash. Cooking with the seasons is one of the great challenges and pleasures of Spa cooking. Also, don't forget about fresh herbs—you will find them amazingly vivid and aromatic compared to their paler dried equivalents. Some to try: coriander, lemongrass, summer savory, and, of course, sweet basil.

### MEAT AND FISH

A cardinal rule in shopping for meat, poultry, and fish is: get to know your butcher (or fish dealer). Someone who knows you and who knows you care about what you buy is more likely to give you good information and to remember you when you call in an order. It also helps to know what you are buying. The cuts of veal and poultry used in Spa recipes are quite straightforward and can be purchased easily at any good butcher shop.

When buying fresh fish, remember that it should not smell fishy. If possible, inspect a fish before it is filleted: the eyes should be bright, not clouded or opaque, the gills should be bright red, and the flesh should be firm to the touch. In purchasing fillets that are already cut, you are more at the mercy of your fishmonger. If he fails you, let him know—and find another fish store.

### DAIRY PRODUCTS

At the Spa we do not serve many dairy products, and most of those we do include are low-fat—low-fat yogurt instead of sour cream, low-fat milk instead of heavy cream, etc. Sometimes, though, there is no substitute for the real thing; for instance, some dishes are sautéed in a small amount of unsalted butter, never margarine.

We recommend using fertile eggs—that is, eggs that have been fertilized by a rooster and produced by free-range hens. Not only are these eggs more nutritious, their taste is incomparably better. Fertile eggs, labeled as such, are available in many health-food stores and in some supermarket chains.

### BAKED GOODS

At the Spa we use a delicious 100 percent whole-wheat bread made with rye flour and sprouted wheat. With a bit of sleuthing you should be able to find several delicious and wholesome whole-wheat breads at health food stores and many bakeries; simply be sure they are made of 100 percent whole wheat (no white flour, unbleached or otherwise), free of preservatives and additives, and low in added sugars and salt. For industrious cooks, we've included a recipe for a tasty wheat bread that freezes beautifully (page 82).

## THINGS TO HAVE ON HAND

Buy these ingredients in small quantities so that you can keep them as fresh as possible:

**Stone-ground whole-wheat flour** and **stone-ground whole-wheat pastry flour; bran flakes** (also called miller's bran); **raw wheat germ** (preferably in vacuum-sealed jars); **baking powder without aluminum** (Rumford is one brand); **roasted carob powder; unsweetened desiccated** (shredded) **coconut; vanilla beans.**

### GRAINS AND LEGUMES

**Rolled oats, whole-wheat berries** (also called whole-grain wheat), **bulgur, wild rice, lentils, brown rice, split peas, navy beans, barley, kidney beans, white lima beans.**

### OILS

Cold-pressed vegetable oils, such as olive oil or safflower oil, are best, and they are the only type we use at the Spa.

Recent research has shown that rancid fats and oxidized fats can produce "free-radical" molecules that may contribute to skin wrinkling and cancer. To prevent fats from spoiling, buy your oil in small quantities and keep it refrigerated. Try one or more of the varieties listed below to see which suits your palate best, and always buy the highest-quality oil available:

**Peanut oil, safflower oil, olive oil, walnut oil, extra-virgin olive oil** (made from the olive's first pressing), **almond oil.**

## NUT BUTTERS

Supermarket peanut butter usually contains hydrogenated oils, sugar, and salt. Find nut butters made without additives, and keep them refrigerated.

**Cashew butter** (raw or toasted), **toasted almond butter, peanut butter** (chunky or smooth), and **sesame butter** (tahini) are available at most gourmet and all Middle Eastern food stores.

## SWEETENERS

In lieu of refined sugar, we use the natural sugars listed here, as well as liberal doses of such natural sweeteners as dates, reduced fruit juices, and fruit purées. Just keep in mind that while the sweeteners listed here are natural, they are still not low-calorie. Think of all refined sugars as poison, and avoid chemical sweeteners.

**Barley malt sweetener, date sugar, uncooked (raw) honey, blackstrap molasses.**

## BEVERAGES

**Bottled spring water** (either sparkling or noncarbonated), **unsweetened fruit juices** such as Concord grape, pomegranate, and apple, **herbal teas of assorted flavors,** including almond and orange.

## MISCELLANEOUS

**Noninstant dried skim milk:** smell before you use, to make sure that it is fresh.

**Vegetable seasoning,** a salt substitute made from dried herbs and vegetables, soy protein, and various enzymes. The seasoning is marketed under several brand names and is widely available in all health-food stores.

**Wasabi** (powdered Japanese horseradish) is used as a seasoning for sashimi, raw fillets of fish served Japanese style. It is available in tubes of paste, which are ready to use, or powdered, which must be reconstituted with water.

**Tofu,** also called bean curd, is now widely available packaged in water at supermarkets. It is also sold by the cake at many greengrocers.

Tofu comes in two varieties: soft tofu, which comes in large porous blocks and crumbles easily, and firm tofu, silkier, denser cakes that can be sliced readily. Recipes will specify which type is needed.

**Low-sodium soy sauce.**

**Vinegars,** including rice vinegar, available at Oriental markets, and flavored vinegars (such as thyme or raspberry vinegar), found at specialty stores.

# COOKING EQUIPMENT

Cooking Spa food at home requires very little special equipment. Sharp knives, a vegetable parer, a colander, a salad spinner, mixing bowls, heavy skillets, and a good assortment of pots, including a stockpot, are part of the *batterie de cuisine* of most households. Some of our recipes recommend using nonstick skillets or baking pans. Although not absolutely essential, nonstick pans will allow you to cook virtually without grease, and one or two skillets, two 8-inch loaf pans, and a baking sheet would be particularly useful to have.

There are several pieces of equipment that are so helpful in the preparation of Spa recipes that they can be considered essential.

A food processor purées soups and sauces and chops vegetables in seconds. The slicing, julienning, and shredding blades make all those chores a breeze.

A blender is wonderful for producing frothy drinks and sauces and is good for puréeing small quantities of soft food.

An electric juicer, as distinct from a citrus juicer, is essential for making fresh fruit and vegetable drinks and is a worthwhile investment. The juicer will emulsify carrots and apples.

There are seven Spa desserts for which an immersion blender is required. It is the only machine capable of transforming nonfat skim milk into whipped cream. If you are a lifetime dieter, an immersion blender will open up a whole new world of desserts. The blender consists of a handheld deep metal beaker and a shaft to which a whipping nozzle is attached.

An electric or hand-powered ice cream freezer is necessary to make Honey-Vanilla Ice Cream (page 51) and will readily whip up our luscious Spa sorbets. The sorbets can also be made by puréeing the frozen mixture in a food processor, but the texture will not be quite as fluffy or "authentic" as sorbet made in an ice cream freezer.

With an electric yogurt maker you can make homemade, foolproof yogurt every time.

A mandoline for shredding and julienning firm vegetables saves lots of time at the chopping board and makes a cleaner cut than food processor blades. Owning a mandoline will encourage you to try recipes you might otherwise not attempt.

# INDEX

**A**corn squash purée, 150
Aïoli, artichokes with, 130
Almond-pineapple blend, nutty, 18
Anjou pears with orange zabaglione, 87
Apple
    butter, honeyed, 38
    -carrot concoction, 14
    cider, New England hot spiced, 91
    -cinnamon muffins with yogurt, 22
    cobbler, old-fashioned hot, 67
    sorbet, 55
    and walnut salad with honey-yogurt
        dressing, 146
Apricot and prune compote, hot oatmeal with
        yogurt and, 74
Artichokes
    with aïoli, 130
    with chickpea salad and lemon mayonnaise,
        99
Arugula, romaine, and red leaf lettuce salad,
    127
Asparagus
    cold poached salmon with endive and, 55
    with lemon dressing, 42

**B**anana(s)
    baked, with orange sauce, 79
    -papaya smoothie, 15
Barbecue menu, 124–127
Barbecue sauce, 126
Barley and split pea soup, hearty, 67
Basil sauce, 47
Bass, Provençal, poached, with garden
        vegetables, 86
Bean(s)
    green, grilled swordfish with new potatoes
        and, 26–27
    pinto, chili, 127
    and potato salad, dilled, 130–131
    refried, chicken coriander tostada with, 39
    three-, salad with fresh coriander, 134
Beverages, 165
    blueberry-nectarine smoothie, 19
    California citrus juice, 15
    carrot-apple concoction, 14
    cucumber-mint frappe, 15
    grapefruit-tangerine juice, 19
    herbal teas, 119
    iced cappuccino, 47
    mineral water, 118–119, 154
    New England hot spiced apple cider, 91
    nutty almond-pineapple blend, 18
    orange-strawberry frappe, 18
    papaya-banana smoothie, 15
    pineapple-lime purée, 14
    at social gatherings, 118–119
    Sonoma Valley red wine spritzer, 102
    sparkling Sonoma white wine spritzer, 58
    sunset spritzer, 127
    sweet sesame nightcap, 19

    vegetable broth, 15
    watermelon-lime cooler, 131
Bibb and red leaf lettuces vinaigrette, 46
Blackberry sorbet, 35
Blenders, 165
Blueberry
    mousse, 43
    -nectarine smoothie, 19
Borscht, hot, 134
Bran muffins, Sonoma, 98
Breads, 164
    cinnamon-orange poppy seed, 38
    Grandma's whole-wheat, 82
    see also muffins
Breakfast crêpes with fresh strawberry purée
        and orange-yogurt sauce, 90
Briefcase lunch menu, 112–115
Broccoli
    lemon-, whole boiled lobsters with wild rice
        and, 70–71
    salad with lemon-mustard dressing, 134
Brochettes, Indian chicken, with lentils and
        snow peas, 78
Broth
    saffron-tomato fish, 87
    vegetable, 15
Brunch menu, 120–123
Brussels sprouts, rosebud, 150
Buffet dinner menu, 136–139
Bulgur with ginger and scallions, 91
Butters
    herb, fondue, 95
    honeyed apple, 38
    honeyed pear, 82
    see also nut butters; peanut butter

**C**abbage leaves, stuffed, 107
Caesar salad, Jack's, 102
Cantaloupe sorbet, 35
Cappuccino, iced, 47
Carob
    -coconut truffles, 111
    -maple mousse, 31
Carrot
    -apple concoction, 14
    salad, sweet, 115
    soup, curried, with chives, 94
Cashew-date butter, chewy, 46
Celery
    hearts, braised, 139
    stuffed with herbed cheese, 142
Champagne-mango ice cream soda, 51
Cheese
    Gruyère and Swiss chard spread, 143
    herbed, celery stuffed with, 142
Chef's salad, Spa, 23
Cherry tomatoes filled with crisp diced
        vegetables, 142
Chicken
    breasts with wild rice, 58

    brochette, Indian, with lentils and snow peas,
        78
    cold lemon-garlic, 131
    coriander tostada with refried beans, 39
    sauce, shallot-scented, 162
    stock, 161
Chickpea salad, artichokes with lemon
        mayonnaise and, 99
Chili, piquant pinto bean, 127
Cider, apple, New England hot spiced, 91
Cinnamon
    -apple muffins with yogurt, 22
    -orange poppy seed bread, 38
    -orange sorbet, sweet, 23
Citrus juice, California, 15
Cleansing days, 10–11, 12–19
Cocktail party menu, 140–143
Cocktails, 118–119, 154–155
    Sonoma Valley red wine spritzer, 102
    sparkling Sonoma white wine spritzer, 58
Coconut-carob truffles, 111
Coffee-rum zabaglione, 111
Compotes
    apricot and prune, hot oatmeal with yogurt
        and, 74
    hot Italian plum, 83
Concord grape mousse, 75
Cookies
    oatmeal, 114, 115
    peanut butter, 135
Cooking equipment, 165
Crab, San Francisco deviled, 115
Cranberry
    -mushroom stuffing, 147
    -raspberry mousse, 71
Cream, Spa, 27
Crêpes
    breakfast, with fresh strawberry purée and
        orange-yogurt sauce, 90
    Spa, 90
Crudités, seasonal, 70
Cucumber
    -mint frappe, 15
    rounds, scallop seviche on, 143
    soup with fresh dill, cold, 50
Curried carrot soup with chives, 94
Curry sauce, 79
Custard, Spa, with maple syrup sauce, 110

**D**airy products, 164
    see also cheese; eggs; yogurt
Date-cashew butter, chewy, 46
Deep green vegetable terrine, 106
Desserts, 109–111
    Anjou pears with orange zabaglione, 87
    coconut-carob truffles, 111
    coffee-rum zabaglione, 111
    flamed strawberries, 139
    fresh fruits, 114, 115, 131
    fresh fruits on skewer with raspberry
        mousse, 59

fresh peach shortcake à la crème, 27
Grand Marnier soufflé, 103
honey-vanilla heart with raspberry purée, 110
honey-vanilla ice cream, 51
hot Italian plum compote, 83
mango-champagne ice cream soda, 51
New Orleans baked bananas with orange sauce, 79
oatmeal cookies, 114, 115
old-fashioned hot apple cobbler, 67
peanut butter cookies, 135
Spa cream topping, 27
Spa custard with maple syrup sauce, 110
Sap génoises, 95, 115
tropical fruit soup, 111
warm honey-glazed pineapple, 99
see also mousses; sorbets
Dill
    fresh, cold cucumber soup with, 50
    potato and bean salad with, 130–131
    -yogurt sauce, 42
Dips
    creamy Roquefort, 70
    hummus, 142
Dressings, 154
    fresh herb and garlic, 26
    honey-yogurt, 146
    lemon, 42
    lemon mayonnaise, 99
    lemon mustard, 135
    raspberry vinaigrette, 86
    Spa vinaigrette, 23
    see also sauces

**E**ggs, 164
    baked, 30
    poached, 30, 66
    ranchero, 106
    soft-boiled, 30
    Sonoma frittata, 82
Endive
    cold poached salmon with asparagus tips and, 55
    romaine, and watercress salad, 67
    and watercress salad, 139
Enoki mushrooms, spinach salad with, 26
Exercise, 7, 155–159
    aerobic, 156–158

**F**all holiday dinner, 144–151
Fish, 164
    baked oysters, 122
    broth, saffron-tomato, 87
    cold paupiettes of sole with herb mayonnaise, 138
    cold poached salmon with asparagus tips and endive, 55
    grilled shrimp and vegetables with dilled yogurt sauce, 42–43
    grilled swordfish with green beans and new

potatoes, 26–27
    halibut steamed in lettuce leaves with new potatoes, 50
    poached bass Provençal with garden vegetables, 86
    salmon and tuna sashimi, 143
    San Francisco deviled crab, 115
    seafood sausages, 94
    skewered shrimp and sea scallops with eggplant and peppers, 126
    stock, 160–161
    terrine, herb-flecked, 134–135
    whole boiled lobsters with wild rice and lemon-broccoli, 70–71
Flamed strawberries, 139
Fondue, herb butter, 95
Food processors, 165
"Free foods," 63
Frittata, Sonoma, 82
Fruits, 164
    fresh, 114, 115, 131
    fresh, on skewer with raspberry mousse, 59
    summer basket, 38
    tropical, soup, 111
    see also specific fruits

**G**arlic and fresh herb dressing, 26
Garlicky tomato sauce, 75
Gazpacho, 18–19
Génoises, Spa, 95, 115
Giblet gravy, 150
Grains, 164
    bulgur with ginger and scallions, 91
    see also oatmeal
Grand Marnier soufflé, 103
Grandma's whole-wheat bread, 82
Granola, crunchy, with strawberries and milk, 54
Grape, Concord, mousse, 75
Grapefruit
    and fresh mint coupe, 46
    sorbet, 35
    -tangerine juice, 19
Gravy, giblet, 150
Green beans, grilled swordfish with new potatoes and, 26–27
Gruyère and Swiss chard spread, 143

**H**alibut steamed in lettuce leaves with new potatoes, 50
Herb
    butter fondue, 95
    -flecked fish terrine, 135
    and garlic dressing, 26
Honey
    -apple butter, 38
    -glazed pineapple, warm, 99
    -pear butter, 82
    -vanilla heart with raspberry purée, 110
    -vanilla ice cream, 51
    -yogurt dressing, 146

Horseradish sauce, savory, 103
Hummus dip, 142

**I**ce cream, honey-vanilla, 51
Ice cream freezers, 165
Ice cream soda, mango-champagne, 51
Iced cappuccino, 47
Immersion blenders, 165
Indian chicken brochette with lentils and snow peas, 78
Ingredients, 5, 62–63, 164–165
Italian dishes
    California minestrone, 83
    garlicky tomato sauce, 75
    salad, 130
    Spa pesto, 83
    stuffed zucchini, 74–75
Italian plum compote, hot, 83

**J**am, strawberry, homemade, 66
Juicers, 165

**L**eek and potato soup with chives, 78
Legumes, 164
Lemon
    dressing, 42
    -garlic chicken, cold, 131
    mayonnaise, 99
    mustard dressing, 135
    sorbet, 35
Lentils, Indian chicken brochette with snow peas and, 78
Lettuce
    halibut steamed in, with new potatoes, 50
    see also salads
Lime
    -pineapple purée, 14
    -pineapple sorbet, 35
    sorbet, 35
    -watermelon cooler, 131
Lobsters, whole boiled, with wild rice and lemon-broccoli, 70–71

**M**andarin orange sorbet, 35
Mandolines, 165
Mango
    -champagne ice cream soda, 51
    sorbet, 35
Maple
    -carob mousse, 31
    syrup sauce, 110
Marinade, pomegranate juice, 126
Mayonnaise
    lemon, 99
    saffron, 55
    Spa, 43
Meats, 164
    see also chicken; poultry; veal
Melon
    balls, strawberries and, with fresh mint, 98
    sorbet, 35

Mineral water, 118–119, 154
Minestrone, California, 83
Mint
   -cucumber frappe, 15
   and grapefruit coupe, 46
Mousses
   blueberry, 43
   carob-maple, 31
   Concord grape, 75
   cranberry-raspberry, 71
   pumpkin, 151
   raspberry, fresh fruits on skewer with, 59
Muffins
   Sonoma bran, 98
   spicy cinnamon-apple, with yogurt, 22
Mushroom(s)
   -cranberry stuffing, 147
   enoki, spinach salad with, 26
   shiitake, fillet of veal with, 34
   -veal sauce, 163
   and wilted spinach salad, 122–123
Mustard
   -lemon dressing, 135
   Pommery, purée of pineapple and, 27

Nectarine-blueberry smoothie, 19
Nut butters, 164–165
   chewy cashew-date, 46
   see also peanut butter
Nuts
   almond-pineapple blend, 18
   mixed, seeds and, 15, 19
   see also walnuts

Oatmeal
   cookies, 114, 115
   hot, with prune and apricot compote and
     yogurt, 74
Oils, 164
Orange
   -cinnamon poppy seed bread, 38
   -cinnamon sorbet, sweet, 23
   mandarin, sorbet, 35
   sauce, New Orleans baked bananas with, 79
   sorbet, 35
   -strawberry frappe, 18
   -yogurt sauce, 90
   zabaglione, Anjou pears with, 87
   -Zinfandel sorbet, 123
"Out" list, 63
Oysters, baked, 122

Papaya
   -banana smoothie, 15
   filled with fresh summer fruits, 22
Pasta
   primavera with basil sauce, 47
   salad, cold herbed, 114
Pâté, walnut, 91
Peach shortcake à la crème, 27
Peanut butter, 164

cookies, 135
   with sesame, 30
Pear(s)
   Anjou, with orange zabaglione, 87
   butter, honeyed, 82
Peas
   split, and barley soup, 67
   see also snow peas
Pesto, 83
Picnic menu, 128–131
Pineapple
   -almond blend, nutty, 18
   -lime purée, 14
   -lime sorbet, 35
   -Pommery mustard purée, 27
   warm honey-glazed, 99
Pinto bean chili, piquant, 127
Pizza, Spa, 106
Plum, Italian, compote, 83
Pomegranate juice marinade, 126
Poppy seeds
   cinnamon-orange bread, 38
   wafers, 123
Port wine sauce, 138
Potatoe(s)
   and bean salad, dilled, 130–131
   and leek soup with chives, 78
   new, grilled swordfish with green beans and,
     26–27
   new, halibut steamed in lettuce leaves with,
     50
Poultry, 164
   revolutionary roast turkey, 146–147
   rock cornish hens with wild rice stuffing and
     port wine sauce, 138
   see also chicken
Prune and apricot compote, hot oatmeal with
     yogurt and, 74
Pumpkin mousse, 151

Raspberry
   -cranberry mousse, 71
   mousse, fresh fruits on skewer with, 59
   purée, honey-vanilla heart with, 110
   sorbet, 35
   vinaigrette, 86
Ratatouille, Monagasque, 139
Red leaf lettuce
   arugula, and romaine salad, 127
   and Bibb lettuce vinaigrette, 46
Red wine spritzer, Sonoma Valley, 102
Refried beans, chicken coriander tostada with,
     39
Restaurants, dining in, 154–155
Rice, see wild rice
Rock cornish hens with wild rice stuffing and
     port wine sauce, 138
Romaine lettuce
   arugula, and red leaf lettuce salad, 127
   and snow pea salad, 86
   watercress, and endive salad, 67

Roquefort dip, creamy, 70
Rosemary roast veal with fall vegetables, 103
Rum-coffee zabaglione, 111

Saffron
   mayonnaise, 55
   -tomato fish broth, 87
Salads, 154
   arugula, romaine, and red leaf, 127
   Bibb and red leaf lettuces vinaigrette, 46
   chickpea, artichokes with lemon mayonnaise
     and, 99
   cold herbed pasta, 114
   crisp apple and walnut, with honey-yogurt
     dressing, 146
   dilled potato and bean, 130–131
   Italian, 130
   Jack's Caesar, 102
   Minnesota wild rice, 31
   romaine, watercress, and endive, 67
   romaine and snow pea, 86
   Spa chef's, 23
   spinach, with enoki mushrooms, 26
   sweet carrot, 115
   three-bean, with fresh coriander, 134
   watercress and endive, 139
   wilted spinach and mushroom, 122–123
   see also dressings
Salmon
   cold poached, with asparagus tips and
     endive, 55
   and tuna sashimi, 143
Salt substitutes, 165
Sashimi, salmon and tuna, 143
Sauces
   aïoli, 130
   barbecue, 126
   basil, 47
   dilled yogurt, 42
   fresh tomato, with basil and garlic, 59
   garlicky tomato, 75
   herb butter fondue, 95
   maple syrup, 110
   orange-yogurt, 90
   piquant tomato salsa, 39
   port wine, 138
   saffron mayonnaise, 55
   savory horseradish, 103
   shallot-scented chicken, 162
   Spa mayonnaise, 43
   Spa pesto, 83
   veal-mushroom, 163
   see also dips; dressings
Sausages, seafood, 94
Scallop(s)
   sea, skewered with shrimp, eggplant, and
     peppers, 126
   seviche on cucumber rounds, 143
Seafood sausages, 94
Seeds, mixed nuts and, 15, 19
Sesame

nightcap, sweet, 19
-peanut butter, 30
Shallot-scented chicken sauce, 162
Shiitake mushrooms, fillet of veal with, 34
Shortcake, fresh peach, à la crème, 27
Shrimp
 grilled vegetables and, with dilled yogurt
  sauce, 42–43
 skewered with sea scallops, eggplant and
  peppers, 126
Snow peas
 Indian chicken brochette with lentils and, 78
 and romaine salad, 86
Sole, cold paupiettes of, with herb mayonnaise,
 138
Sorbets, 35
 autumn apple, 55
 mandarin orange, 35
 orange-Zinfandel, 123
 pineapple lime, 35
 sweet cinnamon-orange, 23
Soufflé, Gand Marnier, 103
Soups
 California minestrone, 83
 chilled California strawberry, 34
 cold cucumber, with fresh dill, 50
 cold spiced tomato, 114
 curried carrot, with chives, 94
 gazpacho, 18–19
 hearty split pea and barley, 67
 hot borscht, 134
 leek and potato, with chives, 78
 saffron-tomato fish broth, 87
 tropical fruit, 111
 vichyssoise, 122
Spinach
 salad with enoki mushrooms, 26
 wilted, and mushroom salad, 122–123
Split pea and barley soup, hearty, 67
Spritzers
 Sonoma Valley red wine, 102
 sparkling Sonoma white wine, 58
 sunset, 127
Squash
 acorn, purée, 150
 yellow, with shallot butter, 34–35
Stocks, 160–163
 chicken, 161
 fish, 160–161
 veal, 162, 163
 vegetables, 163
Strawberry(ies)
 crunchy granola with milk and, 54
 flamed, 139
 jam, homemade, 66
 melon balls and, with fresh mint, 98
 -orange frappe, 18
 purée, breakfast crêpes with orange-yogurt
  sauce and, 90
 sorbet, 35
 soup, chilled California, 34

Stress management, 158
Stuffing, cranberry-mushroom, 147
Sunset spritzer, 127
Sweeteners, 165
Swiss chard
 and Gruyère spread, 143
 sautéed, 95
Swordfish, grilled, with green beans and new
  potatoes, 26–27

T angerine-grapefruit juice, 19
Teas, herbal, 119
Terrines
 deep green vegetable, 106
 herb-flecked fish, 134–135
Three-bean salad with fresh coriander, 134
Toast, see whole-grain toast
Tofu, 165
Tomato(es)
 broiled, with garlic butter, 51
 cherry, filled with crisp diced vegetabes, 142
 -saffron fish broth, 87
 salsa, piquant, 39
 sauce, garlicky, 75
 sauce with basil and garlic, 59
 soup, cold spiced, 114
Tostada, chicken coriander, with refried beans,
 39
Tropical fruit soup, 111
Truffles, coconut-carob, 111
Tuna and salmon sashimi, 143
Turkey, revolutionary roast, 146–147

V anilla
 -honey heart with raspberry purée, 110
 -honey ice cream, 51
Veal
 fillet of, with shiitake mushrooms, 34
 loin of, with pomegranate juice marinade,
  126
 -mushroom sauce, 163
 roast, with rosemary and fall vegetables, 103
 stock, 162, 163
Vegetables, 164
 acorn squash purée, 150
 asparagus spears with lemon dressing, 42
 braised celery hearts, 139
 broiled tomatoes with garlic butter, 51
 broth, 15
 crisp diced, cherry tomatoes filled with, 142
 deep green, terrine, 106
 fall, rosemary roast veal with, 103
 garden, poached bass Provençal with, 86
 grilled shrimp and, with dilled yogurt sauce,
  42–43
 Italian stuffed zucchini, 74
 Monagasque ratatouille, 139
 rosebud Brussels sprouts, 151
 sautéed Swiss chard, 95
 sautéed zucchini, 58
 seasonal crudités, 70

stock, 163
stuffed cabbage leaves, 107
whole-wheat berries and scallions, 107
yellow and green, with hummus dip, 142
yellow squash with shallot butter, 34–35
see also salads; specific vegetables
Vichyssoise, 122
Vinaigrette
 raspberry, 86
 Spa, 23
Vineyard lunch menu, 132–135

W afers, poppy seed, 123
Walnut
 and crisp apple salad with honey-yogurt
  dressing, 146
 pâté, 91
Wasabi, 165
Watercress
 and endive salad, 139
 romaine, and endive salad, 67
Watermelon-lime cooler, 131
White wine spritzer, sparkling Sonoma, 58
Whole grain toast
 chewy cashew-date butter on, 46
 with jam, poached eggs and, 66
 peanut-sesame butter on, 30
Whole-wheat berries and scallions, 107
Whole-wheat bread, Grandma's, 82
Wild rice
 chicken breasts with, 58
 salad, Minnesota, 31
 stuffing, rock cornish hens with port wine
  sauce and, 138
 whole boiled lobsters with lemon-broccoli
  and, 70–71
Wine
 port, sauce, 138
 red, spritzer, 102
 white, spritzer, 58

Y ellow squash with shallot butter, 34–35
Yogurt
 crunchy granola with strawberries and, 54
 homemade, 54
 -honey dressing, 146
 hot oatmeal with prune and apricot
  compote and, 74
 -orange sauce, 90
 sauce, dilled, 42
 spicy cinnamon-apple muffins with, 22
Yogurt makers, 165

Z abaglione
 coffee-rum, 111
 orange, Anjou pears with, 87
Zinfandel-Orange sorbet, 123
Zucchini
 Italian stuffed, 74–75
 sautéed, 58

# A C K N O W L E D G M E N T S

To the following people living in the beautiful Sonoma Valley, who were so kind and accommodating in permitting us to enter their lives while working on our Spa book, go our thanks:

Friends *Peter Law* and *Bob Tate* who, with unfailing good humor, allowed a crew to descend upon them day after day, and whose guidance and assistance in the Sonoma Valley were invaluable; the very gracious *Audrey Sterling* and the beautiful *Iron Horse Vineyard*, which must be everyone's dream of the wine country; *Gordon Brown*, who not only let us use his lovely home for pictures but has been a wonderful supporter of the Sonoma Mission Inn and Spa from the very beginning; *Ronald Schwartz* of *Ronald James, San Francisco* for freely lending the wonderful, rare china without a blink; *Tiffany's San Francisco* and the super staff, who managed to make our job worlds easier with their marvelous selection of china, crystal, and silver; *Peri Wolfman* of Wolf-man, Gold and Good, Co.; *Mr. and Mrs. George E. Riley* for the use of their wonderful gardens.

Very special thanks also to everyone who worked so hard to help us realize *Spa Food*:

*Chef Lawrence Elbert*, whose dedicated commitment and culinary expertise is behind the sumptuous fare we serve at the Spa; *Toni Christenson and Terri Richards*, Spa nutritionists, whose assistance was also invaluable in creating our menus; *Judy Knipe*, who refined the *Spa Food* recipes, and *Lynne Roberts* for her semantic expertise; *Andrea Deane* for her sensational food styling and *George Ross* for elegant lighting effects, all fabulously photographed by *Lilo Raymond*; *The Sebastiani Vineyards* family; *Regina Linens of San Francisco* for the use of their finest selection of antique and contemporary linens; *American Airlines* and *Peter Dolora*, whose personnel from the ground to the sky makes flying with them a traveler's dream; all the people at *Clarkson N. Potter* who lent their expertise to making *Spa Food* a success, especially *Gael Towey Dillon* who was equally adept at both her roles as Art Director and book designer, *Carol Southern* and *Pam Krauss* for their extreme patience, guidance, and editorial suggestions, *Michael Fragnito* and *Lynne Arany* for keeping everything on schedule, and *Barbara Marks* for her special efforts. Additional thanks to *Charlie Swerz*, of our interior design team, and the entire staff of the Inn & Spa. A very special thank you to friend *Sam Crocker*, a man of true style who put his life on hold for the months this project took and who gave, gave, gave, not only of his time but of his taste, fabulous disposition, and elegantly stocked cupboards. And last, the most important person, who kept all the above (including me) together, my wife, *Carlene*.

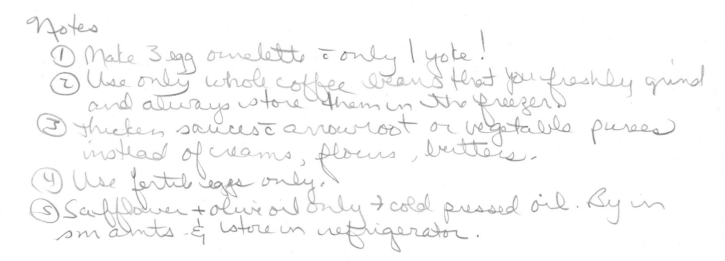

Notes
1. Make 3 egg omelette — only 1 yoke!
2. Use only whole coffee beans that you freshly grind and always store them in the freezer.
3. Thicken sauces — arrowroot or vegetable purees instead of creams, flours, butters.
4. Use fertile eggs only.
5. Safflower + olive oil only — cold pressed oil. Buy in sm amts & store in refrigerator.